✵ INSIGHT POCKET GUIDE

STOCKHOLM

D0351245

C 02 0400043

Part of the Langenscheidt Publishing Group

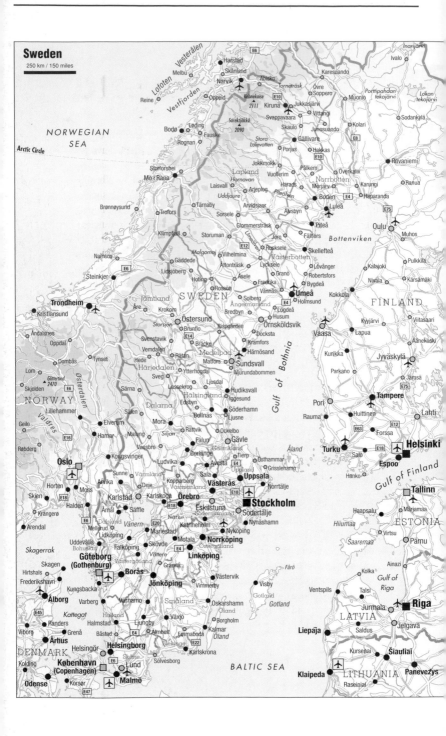

Welcome

This guidebook combines the interests and enthusiasms of two of the world's best-known information providers: Insight Guides, who have set the standard for visual travel guides since 1970, and Discovery Channel, the world's premier source of non-fiction television programming. It brings you the best of Stockholm and its surroundings in 15 itineraries designed by Insight's correspondent in Sweden, Amy Brown. They begin with three full-day tours linking the essential sights, the first exploring the city's ancient roots, from Stadshuset (City Hall) to Gamla Stan (Old Town) and Riddarholmen; the second taking in the art, architecture and history of Norrmalm, Blasieholmen and Skeppsholmen; and the third focusing on the well-preserved bastions of Nordic heritage on the green oasis of southern Djurgården. These are followed by nine short tours, exploring other interesting areas and aspects of the city, and three excursions – to Sweden's ancient capital Uppsala; by steamship on Lake Mälaren to idyllic Mariefred and the Renaissance castle, Gripsholms Slott; and to Utö, an island in Stockholm's outer archipelago, rich in history and rustic charm.

Amy Brown, an American freelance journalist who has lived in Stockholm for 15 years, has contributed to *Insight Guide: Sweden* and *Insight Guide: Scandinavia*. She lived and worked on the East Coast as a newspaper reporter for seven years before meeting her Swedish husband on a summer vacation in Stockholm in 1989. She takes great delight in the history, natural beauty, and magnificent, historic waterside setting of her adopted city, understanding why it continues to be considered one of the most beautiful capital cities of the world. In preparing this Pocket Guide to Stockholm her aim has been to give the visitor a real feel for the city.

She pays due attention to the quintessential sights – the historic Gamla Stan, Skansen, the world's first open-air museum, and the museums of Blasieholmen and Skeppsholmen, which capture the best of Scandinavian art, architecture and design. She is also keen to introduce the visitor to the culinary delights, sophisticated shopping and lively night scene that has made this classic city into such a vibrant hot spot.

6 **contents**

HISTORY AND CULTURE

An introduction to Stockholm's history and culture, from its foundation in 1252, through its 17th- and 18th-century heyday, the years of poverty and mass emigration and on to the industrialisation that led to today's city.............**11**

CITY ITINERARIES

These tours link the finest sights in order of priority. The first three are designed for visitors with only three days to spare; all cover fascinating aspects of the city.

EXCURSIONS

Three worthwhile excursions that are within easy reach of the city.

LEISURE ACTIVITIES

CALENDAR OF EVENTS

PRACTICAL INFORMATION

MAPS

INDEX AND CREDITS

Pages 2/3: view from the tower of the Stadshuset
Pages 8/9: celebrating Midsummer's Eve at Skansen

&*History* &*Culture*

The Vikings, the first people to conquer what is now Sweden, were kept busy by trading, raiding and migratory expeditions throughout the 9th and 10th centuries. As they kept no written history, their triumphs are recorded only in legend and saga, and on the inscriptions of rune stones. Hundreds of thousands of objects found in Viking graves and settlements confirm the extent of their travels. Much of their history is concentrated at Uppsala, an hour from Stockholm, which contains the site of Sweden's last heathen temple – and which was the base for the Svea tribe, which gave its name to Sweden (or Sverige, the Realm of the Sveas) – and at Birka, on the island of Björkö west of Stockholm.

The generally accepted founder of Stockholm is the 13th-century regent Birger Jarl, who wanted to build a fortress to protect Lake Malären against invading pirates. Icelandic literature describes a barrier of piles (logs, or *stock*, in Swedish) across a waterway (*sund*), Stocksundet. The island formed by this piling became known as Stockholm. The largest city in Sweden, it became the capital only when the German-dominated Hanseatic League recognised its importance as a port. The League played a major role in Sweden's foreign trade from the 13th century until the late 17th century.

In 1397, Sweden, Denmark and Norway signed the Kalmar Union (Finland was still part of Sweden). The union was characterised by internal tensions – at the battle of Brunkeberg in Stockholm in 1471, the Danish king tried to take control of Sweden but was defeated by the regent, Sten Sture. The Danes staged another campaign in 1520 which culminated in the notorious Stockholm Bloodbath at Stortorget, when more than 80 noblemen were beheaded.

The Vasa Era

A young nobleman, Gustav Eriksson, whose father and several relatives were murdered in the Stockholm Bloodbath, had the central role in wresting power from the Danes. At the end of 1520, Gustav and his army ousted the Danish King Kristian from Sweden and, on June 6 1523 (which became Sweden's National Day), he was named king, with the title Gustav Vasa.

King Gustav Vasa is also known as the 'nation builder' after the crucial part he played in founding modern Sweden. When he took the throne, the country was in a financial crisis, so he asked parliament to pass a controversial law transferring the property of the Church to the state. This led to a gradual separation from Catholicism and the adoption of the Lutheran State Church. Vasa also decreed, in 1544, that the monarchy should be hereditary.

Gustav Vasa's descendants ruled during the period that Sweden became one of Europe's great powers. His son, Erik XIV, waged wars against

Left: Stockholm in medieval times
Above: Viking artefacts reveal much about the country's first conquerors

Denmark, Lubeck and Poland. His brothers dethroned him and he died in prison, in 1577, reportedly poisoned with pea soup by his brother Johan III. During the reign of the third son, Karl XII, the country waged war against Denmark and Russia. Gustav II Adolf ascended the throne in 1611, and during his reign Sweden steadily increased its dominance over the Baltic region. The king decided to intervene in the Thirty Years' War, with the pretext of religious motives. He was killed at the battle of Lutzen in 1632.

Gustav II Adolf's only child, Kristina, was a mere six years old when he died. Kristina became queen in 1644. During her reign, life at the court was influenced greatly by the world of science and philosophy. Among the well-known scholars who spent time at the Swedish royal court was the French philosopher and mathematician René Descartes (1596–1650). Kristina showed impressive political skills, but her unwillingness to marry and thereby ensure the succession created problems. Having managed to have her cousin Karl Gustav appointed heir in 1650, she abdicated four years later. She left for Rome, where she converted to Catholicism.

Karl X Gustav was a skillful military commander – one of his most famous successes was the victory over the Danes in 1658. The Swedish army advanced to Copenhagen after the king suddenly decided to march his soldiers across the Great Belt, which was frozen in the course of an unusually severe winter. Had the ice on the straits cracked under the weight of the Swedish army, the country would have suffered a disastrous military defeat, but it didn't. The king secured the southern Swedish provinces and divided the land more evenly between the crown, nobility and peasants.

Defeat at Poltava

In 1697 Karl XI died (while his body lay in state at Tre Kronor Castle, a fire destroyed most of the building) and the monarchy fell to the 15-year-old Karl XII. The young king faced an overwhelming task when Denmark, Poland and Russia formed an alliance in 1700 with the purpose of crushing Swedish power. The king forced Denmark and Poland to sue for peace, but he was less successful with Russia, whose army routed the Swedes at Poltava in 1709. This landmark battle marked the beginning of the end of Sweden's era as a great power. Karl XII returned in 1715 after an absence of 15 years but he never succeeded in returning his country to the power it had enjoyed in the 17th century. He was eventually killed in Norway in 1718. At the time of his death, Sweden was in a state of crisis. Crop failures and epidemics had destroyed one-third of Stockholm's population and the state's finances were completely drained.

Karl XII remains the most controversial of Sweden's monarchs. Some praise and admire this warrior king while others condemn him for the series of disasters that plagued the country during his reign. Over the centuries he has often been used as a symbol during patriotic demonstrations, and the anniversary of his death (November 30) is still celebrated in some parts of Sweden, not least by extreme nationalist groups.

Left: Gustav II Adolf

The Age of Liberty

Karl XII did not marry and had no heirs. His sister Ulrika Eleonara was elected monarch but only a year or so later she was succeeded by her husband, Frederik of Hesse. The subsequent 50 years of Swedish history are referred to as the Age of Liberty. Royal absolutism had ended, at least for the time being. In 1719 a new constitution greatly weakened the power of the king. The Age of Liberty coincided with Europe's Enlightenment, which saw dramatic advances in culture, science and industry. The botanist Carl von Linné and the scientist and philosopher Emmanuel Swedenborg became two of the most famous Swedes of their time. Industry, particularly textiles, expanded, more land was placed under cultivation and the first hospital was constructed on Kungsholmen to meet the needs of the growing city.

King Gustav III was crowned in 1772 after a bloodless coup, and he want a long way to restoring royal absolutism. Impressed by French culture and Enlightenment thinking, he played a significant role in the evolution of Swedish cultural life. He was a patron of the arts with a particular affinity for literature, music and art, and in 1786 he founded the Swedish Academy, modelled on its French counterpart. Since 1901 the academy has selected the winners of the annual Nobel Prize in literature. (The inventor and philanthropist Alfred Nobel [1833–96] established the prize the year before he died.)

Over the years opposition to the king's absolute power grew, due in part to the costly war against Russia. In 1792 he was murdered by a nobleman, Captain Anckarström, during a masked ball at the Opera House – a building whose construction he had ordered. Gustav III was succeeded by his son, Gustav IV Adolf, in whose reign, Sweden could not help but become involved in the Napoleonic Wars. After a war against Russia in 1808–9, Sweden lost sovereignty over Finland, which at the time made up one-third of Swedish territory. As a result, the king abdicated and fled the country.

By the early 19th century, the absolute power of the monarch had been consigned to history. The aristocracy suffered a blow in 1809 when a new

Above: Karl XII's army beats a retreat

constitution divided power between government and parliament. A new middle class had emerged and wanted its voice to be heard.

The difficulty of finding a suitable heir to the throne led, in 1810, to the sensational choice of one of Napolean's marshals, Jean-Baptiste Bernadotte. He took the name of Karl XIV Johan when he assumed the throne eight years later. The founder of the present royal dynasty, Karl XIV Johan continued to speak French – he never bothered to learn the Swedish language. But in 1813 he led a Swedish army to victory at the Battle of Leipzig, which forced Denmark to hand over Norway to Sweden. The Norwegeians weren't exactly happy about being ruled from Stockholm, but the union lasted until 1905.

Industrialisation

The 19th century was generally a peaceful period in Sweden, and it was marked by a dramatic population increase. Within a few years, the number of Swedes grew by a million; by 1850, the country's population numbered 3.5 million. Poverty was rife, not only due to the prevalence of crop failures but because there was simply not enough employment. Mass emigration ensued: from the 1850s to the 1930s about 1.5 million Swedes left their homeland, most of them for North America, in search of a better life.

Sweden's transformation from an agricultural society into an industrialised country helped overcome the problems posed by the population surplus. The industrial revolution gained momentum in the late 19th century with the textile, timber and iron industries providing the main sources of employment. The city was characterised during this era by folk movements that retain their place in Swedish life today. Against a backdrop of widespread alcoholism, the temperance movement encouraged abstinence

from the demon drink. In the 1820s annual consumption of spirits was at least five times higher than today. Households were allowed to distill *brännvin*, a traditional plain or flavoured vodka, for their own consumption, but in 1860, under pressure from the temperance society, this right was withdrawn by parliament. Still today, spirit sales are controlled by the state liquor monopoly.

Despite the mass emigration to America, Sweden's population reached 5 million by 1900. As was the case in other industrialising countries, peasants were moving to the towns and cities; by the early 20th century Stockholm's population was about 300,000 – a fourfold increase since 1800.

As the Social Democrat and Liberal parties rose to power in the early 20th century, the demand for universal suffrage was joined by radical authors such as August Strindberg. This was granted for both sexes in 1921. By then the reigning king, Gustav V, had been forced to accept that it was not his but parliament's prerogative to determine the country's form of government.

The Welfare State

In 1936 the Social Democrats and the Farmers' Party formed a far-reaching alliance: together they developed the welfare state, guaranteeing economic security for all. Reforms included unemployment benefit, paid holidays and childcare, and the right to good housing. Poverty was effectively eliminated during the 1930s and 1940s. In 1939, when World War II broke out, Sweden declared its neutrality. The Social Democrats dominated the political scene from the 1930s to the 1970s, in which time non-socialist power blocs ensured a political balance within the government.

During the Cold War, Sweden adopted a policy of non-alignment, which is not to be mistaken for non-involvement. The country's most famous prime minister, Olof Palme (1927–86), was deeply engaged in issues of democracy and disarmament, as well as the problems of the Third World. His assassination on the streets of Stockholm in 1986 shocked the world; the murder remains unsolved.

The final years of the 20th century were a time of significant constitutional change. A new constitution in 1974 removed the monarch's political powers, and in 1995 Sweden joined the European Union after a referendum approved the move by a narrow margin. And the Church severed its link with the state after more than 400 years. At the dawn of the third millennium, rapid technical developments and globalisation are sparking new job opportunities and attracting new inhabitants to Stockholm. Today the city's residents are very conscious of their modern image. Swedish pop music has become an international industry that is generating a new sense of confidence. The city plays a leading international role in information technology and biotechnology. Taking advantage of Stockholmers' reputation for being

Above Left: in Napoleonic times. **Left:** embarking on a new life in the New World
Above: modern Stockholmers are open-minded, trend-hungry and tech-friendly

open-minded, trend-hungry and tech-friendly, fashion houses and IT firms regularly use the city as a testing ground for new products.

Stockholm is a city of growing cultural and social diversity, where waves of immigration have changed the texture of a once homogenous society. This is reflected in the abundance of ethnic restaurants and the international influence on traditional Swedish cuisine. Yet while they love a good meal, a night at the opera, and dancing into the wee hours at trendy nightclubs, even the most sophisticated city-dwellers are happiest when they can swim naked and bond with nature. Much of Stockholm's beauty arises from the fact that only about a third of the city's surface area is concrete and asphalt; the rest is parks and water, and the great outdoors is but a short drive away.

Swedes may at first seem a little cool and formal. But beneath that composed exterior and self-satisfaction with all things Swedish, they are a friendly people – especially after one or two *schnapps*. The unyielding state monopoly on alcohol has created a sense of deprivation that causes many Swedes to over-indulge when they have the chance. Yet when it comes to dining, proper etiquette is in order, from arriving punctually to the smallest of glances exchanged with other dinner guests before and after the traditional toast, or *skål*.

A City that Loves Children

Few major European cities share Stockholm's reputation for welcoming children. You might be surprised to discover how many amenities and how much entertainment is planned around the needs of the youngest inhabitants and visitors. Many of the city's parks allow children to borrow toys, sporting equipment and bicycles at no charge. Parents with pushchairs benefit from 'kneeling' buses and many other services designed with families in mind.

Throughout its rich and varied history the city has shown a remarkable ability to adapt to changing times while creating a vibrancy that is all its own. It could be said that Stockholm never really lost its Viking fervour for the conquest of new worlds. Throughout the city you will see how the old has been fused to the new, often to startling effect.

Above: IT firms often use Stockholm as a testing ground for new products

HISTORY HIGHLIGHTS

1252 Stockholm is first mentioned in a letter by the man usually referred to as its founder, the regent Birger Jarl.

1397 Kalmar Union links the Nordic countries.

1471 Sten Sture the Elder defeats the Danish King Kristian at Brunkeberg.

1520 Swedish noblemen executed in the notorious Stockholm Bloodbath.

1523 Gustav Vasa is chosen as the new king and he marches into Stockholm at the head of an army.

1527 Parliament confiscates Church property during the Reformation.

1560 Gustav Vasa dies.

1561 Erik XIV is crowned king and curbs the power of his brothers. He is later imprisoned by his brothers at Gripsholms Slott and dies in 1577, probably poisoned.

1569 Johan III crowned in Stockholm.

1611 Gustav II Adolf comes to power.

1618 The Thirty Years' War starts in Germany.

1632 Gustav II Adolf killed in battle at Lutzen.

1633 Six-year-old Kristina becomes queen; guardians rule the country.

1654 Kristina abdicates and Karl X Gustav is crowned king. A year later she converts to Catholicism and is ceremonially greeted in Rome.

1697 Tre Kronor Castle destroyed by fire; Karl XII, aged 15, is crowned.

1719 New constitution transfers power from the king to parliament.

1741 Botanist Carl von Linné appointed professor at Uppsala.

1772 The new king, Gustav III, orchestrates a bloodless *coup d'état* that gives the king absolute power.

1786 Swedish Academy founded.

1792 Gustav III murdered.

1809 Sweden loses Finland; Gustav IV Adolf abdicates.

1810 Parliament chooses Jean-Baptiste Bernadotte as Crown Prince.

1814 Sweden gains Norway in peace with Denmark.

1818 Karl XIV Johan crowned king of Sweden and Norway.

1850 Sweden's population rises to 3.5 million (93,000 in the Stockholm area).

1869 Emigration to North America increases due to crop failures.

1876 L M Eriksson starts the manufacture of telephones.

1879 August Strindberg's novel *The Red Room* is published.

1895 Alfred Nobel establishes the Nobel Prize.

1905 Parliament dissolves the union with Norway.

1921 Universal suffrage introduced.

1939 Sweden's coalition government declares neutrality in World War II.

1940 Swedish–German agreement to allow the transit of German military personnel.

1950 First public TV broadcast in Sweden; Stockholm's first underground railway is inaugurated.

1955 Obligatory national health insurance established.

1973 Gustav VI Adolf dies and is succeeded by his grandson, Carl XIV Gustaf.

1974 The monarch loses all political powers.

1986 Prime Minister Olof Palme is murdered in Stockholm. Police fail to catch the culprit.

1995 Sweden joins the European Union after a referendum.

2000 Church separates from the state after 400 years.

2002 Stockholm celebrates its 750th anniversary.

2003 Foreign Minister Anna Lindh murdered in Stockholm.

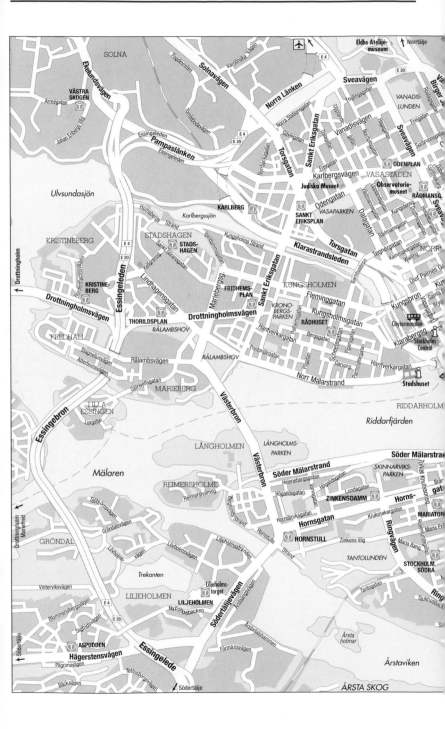

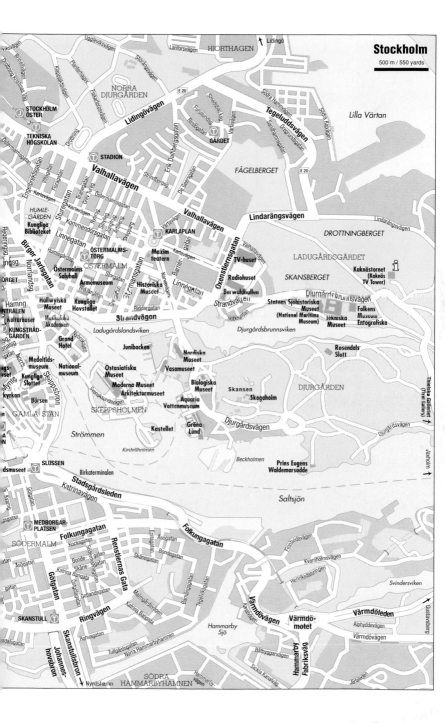

City
Itineraries

1. GAMLA STAN *(see map, p22)*

Starting at the Stadshuset (City Hall) on Kungsholmen, this tour wends its way through the city's oldest quarters, including a stroll past the graceful palaces that house government offices on Helgeandsholmen, to the heart of the ancient city in Gamla Stan, ending with the serene and sparsely populated island of Riddarholmen.

To arrive at Stadshuset at Hantverkargatan, take the subway (T-bana) to T-Rådhuset or buses 3 and 62. Note that the building can be viewed only with a guide. This full-day walking itinerary begins with the 10am tour.

From any part of Stockholm south of Lake Mälaren, **Stadshuset** (guided tours Sept–May: daily 10am, noon; June–Aug: 10am, 11am, noon, 2pm, 3pm) dominates the skyline. On the Riddarfjärden water's edge, this is the master work of architect Ragnar Östberg. A massive, square, 105m (345ft) tower rises from one corner of an elegant central building constructed with decorated brickwork and with an open-fronted portico facing the lake. The building is topped with spires, domes and minarets, and the roofs are clad in a delicate green copper. Above it gleam the Tre Kronor, the three golden crowns that symbolise the country. Östberg began work in 1911 and devoted the next 12 years of his life to Stadshuset. He used 8 million bricks and 19 million gilded mosaic tiles, the latter mostly in the famous Golden Hall. In the gardens of the southern terrace there is a statue of Engelbrekt Engelbrektsson, the 15th-century Swedish patriot who championed the cause of the peasants in his native Dalarna. Climb the tower for one of the best views of the city. A procession depicting the figures of St George and the Dragon emerges twice a day as the bells play a medieval tune.

A Rose Bath By Any Other Name

Leaving Stadshuset, head east past Stadshusbron to the pedestrian walkway along Klara Mälarstrand and then up the steps to Strömgatan, leading to Riksbron. To your right is the imposing **Riksdag**, the House of Parliament, and to your left is **Rosenbad** ('rose bath'), a series of palatial buildings overlooking the Strömmen channel which, since 1981, have housed the Swedish government and the prime minister's private office.

The Jugendstil (Art Nouveau) pink sandstone house on the corner of Fredsgatan and Drottningatan, designed by leading late 19th-century architects, houses the Skåne bank. The Venetian-style palace along Strömgatan, the last to be finished (in 1904), was the site of a bank, flats and a restaurant. Rosenbad took its name from a 17th-century bathhouse that offered lily, camomile and rose baths.

Left: City Hall dominates the skyline
Right: crown on the Skeppsbron

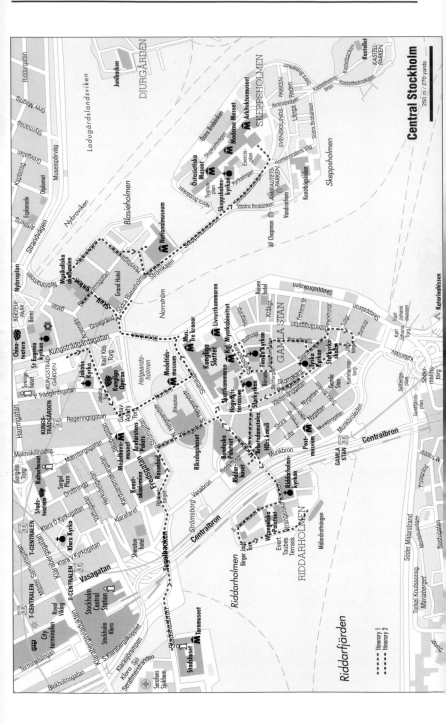

Continue south along Riksgatan to Stallbron, leading to Mynttorget, and then turn right to reach **Riddarhuset** (House of Nobility; Mon–Fri 11.30am–12.30pm), one of four parliamentary estates. This is arguably the most beau-

tiful building in Gamla Stan, with two pavilions looking out across the water. Inside, the erstwhile power of the nobles is reflected by the grandeur of the Main Chamber, where the nobles deliberated, watched from the ceiling by a painting of Mother Svea, who symbolises Sweden.

Leaving Riddarhuset, turn left towards the Kungliga Slottet (Royal Palace), cross Mynttorget and climb up the steps to reach **Högvaktsterassen** where the Royal **Changing of the Guard** takes place daily, shortly after noon. This is one of Stockholm's most popular tourist attractions, so arrive early for a good view. A good choice for lunch is one of the nearby restaurants housed in medieval cellars, either Restaurang Kaffe Gillet at Trångsund 4, opposite Storkyrkan (Great Cathedral) or Café Källaren Sten Sture at Trångsund 10. If you would rather sit outside, there are several cafés and restaurants in Stortorget.

The Oldest Building

After lunch, head back along Trångsund to **Storkyrkan** (daily 9am–4pm; Oct–Nov Sat and Sun only: 9am–6pm). This awesome gothic cathedral is the oldest building in Gamla Stan, part of it dating back to the 12th century. It has high vaulted arches and sturdy pillars stripped back to their original red brick, and a magnificent organ. Storkyrkan's most famous statue,

St George and the Dragon, a wooden affair carved by Bernt Notke in 1489, is the largest medieval monument in Scandinavia. Check out the candelabra (17th-century) and the plaque to the three generations of the Tessin family, who built the Royal Palace.

On leaving the cathedral, walk to Slottsbacken, where you can see a statue of Olaus Petri, the father of the Swedish Reformation. The entrance to the **Kungliga Slottet** palace (Sept–mid-May: Tues–Sun noon–3pm; mid-May–Aug: 10am–4pm) is on Slottsbacken. The palace, built on the site of the Tre Kronor Palace (which burned down in 1697) has 608 rooms, and some of the suites are open to the public. The oldest interiors,

Above: a guard on duty
Right: St George and the Dragon

dating from the 1660s, are in the north wing. The palace is famous for its tapestries, both of Gobelins and Swedish design. The most evocative room is Oskar II's Writing Room in the Bernadotte Apartments. This has been kept exactly as the king left it when he died in 1907; even his desk is untouched. It is a comfortable, pleasant room, full of 19th-century clutter and family photographs.

The Skattkammaren (Treasury) beneath the palace holds the stunning Crown Jewels. Immensely valuable and brilliantly lit, they glow in the dim light of the vaults. Also underground is the Livrustkammaren (Royal Armoury), which has the stuffed remains of the horse of Gustav II Adolf, who extended Sweden's domain as far as Poland before his death on the battlefield of Lutzen in 1632. The palace is also the site of Gustav III's Museum of Antiquities, whose ancient marble sculptures were acquired on the king's journey to Italy, and the Tre Kronor Museum, which depicts the palace before the 1697 fire.

Leaving the palace, walk up Slottsbacken to **Stortorget**, the central square, with narrow streets fanning out in all directions. Today Stortorget is peaceful, but in medieval times it was a crowded, noisy trading centre where German merchants, stallholders, craftsmen and young servant girls and boys jostled and shouted. Along one side is **Börsen**, the old Stock Exchange building, and the modern Stock Exchange still occupies the ground floor. The Swedish Academy meets here to elect the winners of the Nobel Prize for Literature.

Site of the Stockholm Bloodbath

As people laze on benches or enjoy a meal at one of the outdoor cafés, it is hard to imagine that in 1520 the cobbled square ran with blood during the Stockholm Bloodbath, when the Danish King Kristian II murdered 82 people – not only influential noblemen but any civilian unlucky enough to have a shop or a business nearby. In 1523, after taking revenge against Denmark, Sweden's first heroic king, Gustav Vasa, marched into Stockholm.

To begin our leisurely stroll through Gamla Stan, walk down **Köpmangatan**, which in medieval times was the city's main street. Stop at No 11, which still has part of its medieval wall intact (although it has the year 1730 inscribed above the doorway). The portal, with its cherubs and a carved hand holding roses, dates back to the beginning of the 17th century. If you peek in through the glass squares of the doorway you will see a medieval passageway leading to a leafy garden that is open in summer – part of an effort in the 1930s to let more light, air and sun into these closely packed houses.

The Smallest Statue

Retrace your steps on Köpmangatan and turn left onto Trädgårdstvärgrand which leads to the **Finska Kyrka** (Finnish Church) opposite the palace gate. Behind it is **Bollhustäppan** (Ball Court Garden). This little courtyard has flowers, a small fountain, benches and Stockholm's smallest statue, a figure of a seated boy only a few inches high. From here, walk down Trädgårdsgatan to Skeppar Olofs Gränd and cross Köpmansgatan to Själargärdsgatan, where you will come to the tree-lined square of Brända Tomten, named after a house destroyed in a fire. This prompted the city architect to create in its place a much-needed turning zone for fire engines and other vehicles.

Turn right onto Tyska Skolgränd (German School Lane). Together with Tyska Kyrkan (German Church) and Tyska Brinken (German Slope), the lane is a reminder of Germany's overwhelming influence over Stockholm during the 18th century, when the Hanseatic League controlled the Baltic and its ports. The **Tyska Kyrkan** church (May–Aug: daily noon–4pm; Sept–Apr: Sat noon–4pm), founded in 1571, was built in German late-Renaissance and baroque style. Its ebony and alabaster pulpit is unique in Sweden. The altar, dating to the 1640s, is covered with beautiful paintings and is surrounded by sculptures of the evangelists and apostles.

Walk down Svartmangatan to the corner of Baggensgatan (which is named after Admiral Jakob Bagge, 1502–77). Before long you will reach Österlånggatan which, together with Västerlånggatan, used to constitute a ring around the old city wall. Look out for **Den Gyldene Freden**, an artists' restaurant with a long tradition, at Österlånggatan 51. It dates from 1722 and was frequented by Swedish troubadour Carl Michael Bellman. The house and restaurant were donated by the Swedish painter Anders Zorn to the Swedish Academy in 1919. This is an excellent choice for dinner later in the evening. The kitchen serves excellent Swedish/French cuisine as well as modestly priced Swedish home cooking.

Turn left onto Järntorget, which is graced by an amusing statue of Evert Taube (1890–1976), the much-loved popular musician. From here it is short

Above Left: Stortorget takes a turn for the exotic. **Left:** Viewing the Royal Palace
Right: Mårten Trotzigs Gränd, the narrowest street in Gamla Stan

walk along Västerlänggatan to **Mårten Trotzigs Gränd** which, at 90cm (3ft) wide, is the narrowest street in Gamla Stan. Climb up the 36 steps and you will get a good impression of how different parts of Gamla Stan vary in height, and how tightly the houses are packed together. At the top turn left on Prästgatan, a quiet, serene street – in stark contrast to the crowded Västerlånggatan, which is full of tourists, shoppers and strollers. Note in particular No 78 with its baroque portal dating from 1670 and rococo doors from the 1750s. It was here that the painter Carl Larsson was born in 1853.

Monarchs' Tombs

At Storkyrkobrinken, turn left until you reach Riddarhustorget. Next to Riddarhuset you'll see **Bondeska Palatset** (the Bonde Palace) at No 8, the seat of the Supreme Court since 1949, created by architect Nicodemus Tessin the Elder in the style of a French town house. Cross Riddarholmsbron to the quiet island of Riddarholmen. Walk to **Riddarholmskyrkan**, best known

as the place for royal burials (mid May–June and mid Aug–end Aug: daily 10am–4pm; July–mid Aug: 10am–5pm; first half Sept: Tue–Sun noon–3pm; second half Sept: Sat–Sun noon–3pm). The interior is full of ornate sarcophagi, worn gravestones and, in front of the altar, the tombs of the medieval kings Karl Knutsson and Magnus Ladulås. It is built on the site of the late 13th-century Greyfriars Abbey. The vaults contain the remains of all the Swedish monarchs from Gustav II Adolf in the 17th century, with the exception of Queen Kristina, who is buried at St Peter's, Rome, and Gustav VI Adolf, interred at Haga Slott (Haga Castle).

Riddarholmen was once the site of lots of noblemen's residences. **Wrangelska Palatset** at Birger Jarls Torg 16 and Birger Jarls Torn (Birger Jarls Tower) at Norra Riddarholmshamnen both date to the 16th century. Wrangelska Palatset was owned by Carl Gustaf Wrangel, a field marshal in the Thirty Years War, and occupied by the royal family after Tre Kronor Castle burned down. The Court of Appeal now uses the whole building. At Birger Jarls Torg 4 is **Stenbockska Palatset**, the best-preserved nobleman's home on Riddarholmen. It was built in the 1640s by the State Councillor Fredrik Stenbock and the family's coat of arms is visible above the porch. In 1969–71 it was restored as the headquarters of the Supreme Court.

Walk towards Riddarfjärden where Carla's Café has outdoor tables in the summer and a fine view of the water. Close by is Christer Berg's Solbåten (Sun Boat), a graceful granite sculpture that resembles a sail. If you fancy an early dinner or a cocktail, walk a few steps to Mälardrottning, the yacht once owned by American heiress Barbara Hutton, now a hotel and restaurant.

Above: relaxing on the quiet island of Riddarholmen

2. BLASIEHOLMEN AND SKEPPSHOLMEN *(see map, p22)*

Starting in Kungsträdgården, the city's most popular venue for relaxation and entertainment, stroll through the elegant square flanked by the Royal Opera House, and proceed across Strömbron to the 'museum' islands of Blasieholmen and Skeppsholmen, where you can steep yourself in Scandinavian art, architecture and design.

If you are staying in central Stockholm, it's an easy walk to Kungsträdgården, which is opposite the big NK department store on Hamngatan. You can also take the underground to T-Kungsträdgården.

For centuries, **Kungsträdgården** has been the city's most popular meeting place and recreational hub. Stockholmers and tourists alike stroll among the lime trees, admire the lovely fountains and statues, and gather for the many festivals and concerts on the large outdoor stage. In winter, the central skating rink is popular with children and adults. The king's kitchen garden was located here in the 15th century – this is the city's oldest park. In the 16th century, during the reign of Erik XIV, the kitchen plot was transformed into a Renaisssance garden. Queen Kristina later had a stone summer house built in it – you can see this quite lovely 17th-century edifice at Västra Trädgårdsgatan 2 by the cobblestone Lantmäteribacken.

Encircled by avenues, the Strömgatan end of the park leads to Karl XIIs Torg, with J P Molin's statue of the warrior king, sculpted in 1868. Molin also designed the fountain, made from gypsum in 1866 and cast in bronze several years later. Closer to the centre of the park is a statue of Karl XIII (1809–18) by Erik Göthe. Once at the park, you can get coffee at one of any number of cafés along the Kungsträdgårdsgatan side of the park. Café Söderberg at the Strömbron end opens at 8am and the outdoor tables offer a pleasant view.

Just a few metres away, Café Opera, behind the

Above: J P Molin's statue of Karl XII, the warrior king
Right: a lion in Kungsträdgården

Opera House, is an elegant lunch or dining spot as well as nightclub, with a magnificent baroque interior. Walk to your right through Jakobs Torg, past the 16th-century **Jakobs Kyrka**, dedicated to St Jacob, the patron saint of wayfarers. This leads to Gustav Adolfs Torg. The centre of the square features a statue of Gustav II Adolf. On the northeast side is the **Kungliga Operan** (Royal Opera House), first built in 1782 by Gustav III. In 1792, he was murdered during a masked ball at Operan. In the late 19th century, Axel Anderberg was commissioned to design a new opera house when the old building became a fire hazard. The facade is in late-Renaissance style. Inside is a beautiful staircase and paintings by Carl Larsson and Axel Jungstedt. In summer, operas are performed at Drottningholm, but at other times you can enjoy an opera in this regal setting.

An Underground Museum

On the southwest side of the square is **Arvfurstens Palats** (Prince's Palace), which in 1906 was taken over by the Swedish Foreign Office. It was built for Gustav II's sister, Sofia Albertina, and inaugurated in 1794. The palace and decor are classic examples of the Gustavian style. Proceed from the centre of the square southeast across Norrbro, which has the Riksdag (Parliament) on one side and, if you follow the steps down on the east side, the **Medeltidsmuseet** (Medieval Museum), an entirely underground museum built around the capital's archaeological remains. Archaeological digging in the late 1970s revealed part of a city wall dating back to the 1530s. The discovery fortunately put a stop to plans to build a car park on the site. You may want to return here another day to see the museum.

Continue towards the Royal Palace and turn left across Slottskajen then left again onto Strömbron. At the traffic lights turn right onto Strömkajen, where sightseeing boats depart for the city as well as the archipelago. This is the island of Blasieholmen, where a number of elegant palaces were built during the

Above: in the subterranean Medieval Museum
Left: a modern sculpture outside the Modern Museum

country's glory years in the 17th and 18th centuries. Buildings added from the mid-19th century include the National Museum. You can walk to Blasieholmstorg, where two of the city's oldest palaces are separated by two bronze horses. The palace at No 8 was built in the mid-17th century by a field marshal and then rebuilt 100 years later in the style of an 18th-century French palace. It used to host foreign ambassadors and is now known as Utrikesministerhotellet (Foreign Ministry Hotel). The offices of the Musical Academy and Swedish Institute are here. **Bååtska Palatset** stands nearby at No 6. The newly restored exterior dates from 1699, when it was designed by Tessin the Elder. It was partly rebuilt in 1876 for the freemasons, who still have their lodge here.

The Largest Art Collection

At the end of the square, at No 10, note the facade facing onto Nybrokajen, a handsome example of the neo-Renaissance style of the 1870s and 1880s. Turn right onto Nybrokajen and right again onto Hovslagaregatan, which will take you through Musieparken to the entrance of the **National Museum** (Tues, Thur 11am–8pm; Wed, Fri–Sun 11am–5pm). The building, designed in Venetian and Renaissance styles and completed in 1866, houses Sweden's largest art collection, with 16,000 paintings and sculptures. The handicrafts section's 30,000 works cover 500 years and is Scandinavia's largest collection of porcelain. As you climb the upper staircase, you can't miss Larsson's mural *The Entry of King Vasa of Sweden in Stockholm 1523*, or his *Midwinter Sacrifice* on the opposite wall. A new permanent display records a history of design from 1917 to the present, taking in the Stockholm Exhibition (1930), the Scandinavian Design movement (1950s) and Swedish new simplicity (1990s).

As you leave the museum, turn left and cross the wrought-iron Skeppsbron to Skeppsholmen. You'll pass the 100-year-old af Chapman, the sleek schooner which houses a youth hostel and a café. The **Moderna Museet** (Modern Museum, Tues–Wed 10am–8pm, Thur–Sun 10am–6pm; free admission except for special exhibitions) reopened in 2004 after extensive renovation for mould damage. Containing 5,000 paintings, sculptures, 25,000 watercolours, drawings and around 100,000 photographs, its collection of 20th-century international and Swedish art is considered one of the finest in the world. The museum has an espresso bar and a restaurant that serves both light and business lunches.

Museum of Architecture

The **Arkitekturmuseet** (Swedish Museum of Architecture, Tues–Wed 10am–8pm, Thur–Sun 10am–6pm, free admission), shares the entrance to the Moderna Museet. The collection guides visitors through 1,000

Right: a Larsson mural at the National Museum

years of Scandinavian building, from the simplest wooden houses to state-of-the-art techniques and styles. There are models of architectural works worldwide, from 2000BC to the present day. The museum's archive contains 2 million drawings and sketches and 600,000 photographs, all available for visitors to peruse.

An ideal place to enjoy a drink—and, in the summer, a barbecue—is in the quiet garden of Café Bloms next to the Arkitekturmuseet. For dinner choices, walk back over Skeppsbron to the expensive but superb Franska Matsalen (tel: 08-679 35 84) at the Grand Hotel, with an elegant dining room overlooking the Royal Palace, or, especially if you like seafood, go along Nybrokajen to No 17's similarly expensive Wedholms Fisk (tel: 08-611 78 74). For a cheaper option, try Bakfickan (tel: 08-676 5809) in the Operahuset. This favourite of Opera House artists serves Swedish home cooking at the bar and meals from the illustrious Operakällaren's kitchen next door.

3. SOUTHERN DJURGÅRDEN *(see map, p33)*

This tour looks at Nordic history on the lush island of Djurgården, with visits to the palatial Nordiska Museet and the unusual Vasamuseet, which is the home of the *Vasa* warship, and takes a leisurely walk through Skansen, the world's first open-air museum.

To get to the Nordiska Museet, just over Djurgårdsbron, take bus No 44 or 47; in summer you can take either the tram from Norrmalmstorg, or the Djurgårdsfärjen (Djurgårds ferry) from Skeppsbron.

For all its palatial proportions, the Renaissance-style **Nordiska Museet** (Sept–May Mon–Fri 10am–4pm, Sat–Sun 11am–5pm; June–Aug: Mon–Sun 10am–5pm) is only a quarter of its intended size. The building was designed by Isak Gustav Clason and opened in 1907; the museum was created by

city itineraries

Arthur Hazelius (1833–1901), who was also the founder of Skansen *(see page 32)*. In 1872 Hazelius started to collect objects that would preserve the old Nordic farming culture for future generations. Today the Nordiska Museet portrays everyday life in Sweden from the 1520s to the present, with more than 1.5 million exhibits. It's like a grand attic full of treasures, from luxury clothing and priceless jewellery to items such as furniture and children's toys, and replicas of period homes.

As you enter the huge Main Hall, you are greeted by a statue of King Gustav Vasa, carved in painted and gilded oak by Carl Milles (1875–1955) in 1924. Temporary exhibitions are located here. The ground level sections cover guilds, folk costumes and Lapp *(Sami)* culture. On the third floor is the fashion gallery, the Strindberg Collection, dolls' houses, table settings, and traditional items such as the bridal crown. (The Church used to lend such crowns to brides as a symbol of innocence; many Swedish brides still wear a small gold crown atop their veils.) On the fourth floor are sections on furniture, Swedish homes, and small objects. The dolls' houses show typical homes from the 17th century to modern times. A traditional table setting from the 17th century is a feast for the eyes. The Strindberg Collection also includes 16 paintings by the author and dramatist (1849–1912), including *Snowstorm at Sea* (1894). The Lekstugan (Playhouse) on the first floor is a fun place for children to dress up and experience life in the olden days.

The Most Popular Museum

Leaving the museum, turn left and head down Galarvärvsvägen to the **Vasamuseet** (Vasa Museum, daily late Aug–early Jun: 10am–5pm, Wed 10am–8pm; early Jun–late Aug: 9.30am–7pm). This, the city's most popular museum, houses the *Vasa*, the royal warship that capsized in Stockholm's harbour on 10 August 1628 in calm weather after a maiden voyage of just 1,300m (4,265ft). About 50 people died on the ship that was supposed to be the pride of the navy. Only some of the guns could be salvaged from the vessel at the time and it was not until 1956 that the persistence of marine archaeologist Anders Franzén led to the rediscovery of the *Vasa*. After the subsequent salvage operation, the museum opened in 1990 less than a nautical mile from the spot where the *Vasa* sank.

As you walk into the dark interior of the museum, doubtlessly taking in its fragrant wood aroma, you will be immediately struck by the magnificence of the ship, which is amazingly well preserved. The *Vasa* has gold leaf on her poop and bow, guns of bronze, and is decorated with 700 sculptures and carvings. On that August day in 1628 as the *Vasa* set sail from Stockholm, a sudden gust of wind struck. Water flooded through the gun ports, the ship keeled over and sank, drowning all on board. The ballast was

Above Left: enjoying a Kungsträdgården summer festival. **Left:** Djurgårdsvägen
Right: detail of the salvaged *Vasa* at the Vasa Museum

not heavy enough to balance the weight of the heavy artillery on the upper gun deck.

In the salvage operation, described in a film shown by the museum, some 24,000 objects were rescued, including skeletons, sails, cannons, clothing, tools, coins, butter, rum and numerous everyday utensils. You can see many of these objects and some, such as a sailor's *kista* (chest), containing his pipe, shoe-making kit and all the other necessities for a long voyage, are quite poignant.

Leaving the Vasamuseet, walk back up to Djurgårdsvägen and head north 200m/yds, and you will find the entrance to the Blå Porten restaurant. Next to the Liljevalchs Konsthall, it is a lovely place for an alfresco lunch, weather permitting. *Blå porten* means

blue gate, in reference to the time long ago when no one was allowed to enter the royal Djurgården except through the common gates, which were painted blue. **Liljevalchs**, one of Northern Europe's most attractive art galleries, was built in 1913–16 in the then popular neoclassical style.

Gröna Lunds Amusement Park

After lunch, continue south along Djurgårdsvägen past **Gröna Lunds tivoli** (end April–mid Sept, hours vary), an amusement park with roots in the 18th century. If you are travelling with children, or have a weakness for thrills, try to fit this into your itinerary. Among the attractions are a roller-coaster ride, a ferris wheel with great views, a free-fall Power Tower and a brand-new free-fall Tilt Tower, both 80-m (262-ft) towers from which you drop at a terrifying speed. The park has beautiful gardens, 13 restaurants (one with a cabaret), a theatre and three stages that often host world-class performers.

Cross Djurgårdsvägen to the main entrance of **Skansen**. This, the world's first open-air museum (daily May: 10am–8pm; June–Aug: 10am–10pm; Sept: 10am–5pm; Oct–Apr: 10am–4pm) was opened in 1891 by Arthur Hazelius *(see page 31)*, who wanted to preserve the Swedish way of life that was disappearing in the backwash of the Industrial Revolution. Hazelius collected traditional buildings from diverse areas – Skansen features some 150 of them, including an 18th-century church, Seglora Kyrka, which is still used for services and is a popular venue for weddings.

Ascend the escalator up to the Town Quarter, where original Stockholm wooden town houses have been grouped together to

Above and Left: preserving the past at Skansen with period costumes and collected buildings replicate a medium-sized 19th-century town. Glass blowers, shoemakers and other craftsmen demonstrate their traditional skills in restored workshops. The smell of kanelbullar (cinnamon buns) might lure you into the bakery.

Leaving the Town Quarter, walk to Skogaholm Manor, a 17th-century estate from the ironworks village in central Sweden. Stroll to Tingsvallen/Bollnästorget, the venue for the Christmas market and midsummer celebrations, where you can buy the traditional Skansen treat of waffles topped with berry jam and cream. Head east to peer into the Älvros Farmhouse. The living room in this 500-year-old wooden cottage from Härjedalen exhibits the tools used in everyday tasks. In the northern part of the park, Vastveit Loft, a storehouse from eastern Norway, built in the 14th century, is Skansen's oldest building. Skansen also gives a picture of the Swedish countryside and wildlife today. Walk west and you will see brown bears, wolves and elks. Skansen also houses some exotic maritime creatures in its aquarium.

As you wind your way back to the main entrance, be sure to see Hornborga Cottage, a timber building from western Sweden with a straw and peat roof. This demonstrates the living conditions of poorer people in the 19th century.

Boating Options

Leave Skansen by the main Djurgårdsvägen exit, turn left and head back to Djurgårdsbron. The bridge, opened in 1897 for the Stockholm Exhibition, is richly ornamented with cast-iron railings in the form of stylised water plants. Wrought-iron lamps and sculptures of mythical gods sit atop four granite pillars at either end. And there's a grand view of the elegant Strandvägen. Canoes, rowing boats, pedal boats, larger boats and even rollerblades can be hired from Tvillingarnas Båtuthyrning and Skepp & Hoy, both near the bridge, and Djurgårdsbrons Sjöcafé across the bridge. Try Tvillingarnas, a popular floating restaurant, for a drink or meal.

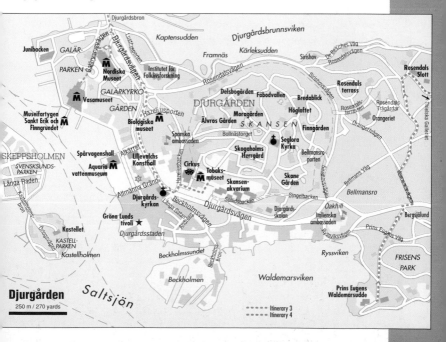

4. NORTHERN DJURGÅRDEN *(see map, p33)*

This tour begins in the centre of the island at the waterfront home and gallery of Prins (Prince) Eugen's Waldemarsudde. It takes in the nearby Rosendal Slott and Trägårdar (gardens) before moving on to Djurgården's northernmost tip to view another private collection of art, this time in the stunning setting of Thielska Galleriet.

To reach Waldemarsudde in summer, hop onto one of the vintage trams (No 7) that leave from Norrmalstorg. Otherwise, bus No 47 will get you there. From Rosendals Slott, you need to walk east about 500m (⅓ of a mile) on Rosendalsvägen to Djurgårdsbrunnsbron to take bus No 69 to Thielska Galleriet (2.5 km/1½ miles from Waldemarsudde). It's also quite feasible to walk to Thielska by heading south on Manillavägen and then east on Djurgårdsvägen. The walk takes about 20 minutes.

Prins Eugen's Waldemarsudde (Tue, Wed, Fri–Sun 11am–5pm, Thur 11am–8pm) is often called the most beautiful gallery in the city, and with good reason. Overlooking Saltsjön, Waldemarsudde was the home of Prins Eugen, the 'painter prince' and brother of the late King Gustav V. Prins Eugen (who died in 1947) bequeathed to the nation his lovely home and garden as well as his collection, which includes a number of impressive landscapes that he painted himself. The prince was trained as a military officer but became one of the foremost landscape painters of his generation. He produced monumental paintings for Kungliga Operan, Kungliga Dramatiska Teatern and Rådhuset. At Waldemarsudde you will find three of his most treasured works: *Spring* (1891), *The Old Castle* (1893) and *The Cloud* (1896).

The Young Ones

The collection is based on the work of Prins Eugen's contemporaries – Swedish artists such as Oscar Björck, Carl Frederik Hill, Richard Bergh, Nils Kreuger, Eugéne Jansson, Bruno Liljefors and Anders Zorn. Prins Eugen was also a generous patron to the next generation of artists, the group known as The Young Ones. The work of this group is represented by artists such as

Issac Grünewald, Einar Jolin, Sigrid Hjertén and Leander Engström. Sculptors from the same era are also represented: you can see works by Per Hasselberg, Carl Milles, Auguste Rodin and Christian Eriksson in both the gallery and the park.

Together with the architect Ferdinand Boberg, Prins Eugen drew up the sketches for the house, which was completed in 1905. The same architect planned the gallery, completed in 1913, that now holds part of the collection of some 2,000 works as well as the prince's own paintings.

Waldemarsudde is renowned for its beautiful indoor flower displays and it is a delightful house to walk through. Check out the white porcelain pots, designed by Prins Eugen, at the entrance. The drawing room and guest apartments remain largely unchanged – one can easily imagine the leisured life, steeped in art, nature, and landscape, that the prince cultivated. The two upper floors, with the prince's studio at the top, are used for temporary exhibitions. You should not leave Waldemarsudde without walking around the beautiful grounds and perhaps stopping for some waffles and coffee in Ektorpet. This small, 18th-century cottage was originally a fisherman's cottage.

Karl Johan Architecture

From Waldemarsudde, head north to Prins Eugens Väg and cross the road, continuing a short distance until you come to Djurgårdsvägen, at which you turn right and then left, heading north, on Valmundsvägen. This leads to Rosendalsvägen and **Rosendals Slott** (June–Aug: Tues–Sun guided tours on the hour noon–3pm). The palace is con-

sidered to be one of the best examples of the Empire or Karl Johan style of architecture, named after King Karl XIV Johan (1818–44). Built and designed in the 1820s as a summer retreat for the king by Fredrik Blom, a popular architect of the time, it was one of Sweden's first prefabricated homes. In 1913 it was opened to the public as a museum devoted to the life and times of Karl XIV Johan, and it remains a highly impressive work of historic restoration.

The decor is magnificent, with Swedish-made furniture and richly woven textiles in brilliant colours. The carpeting and curtains are extraordinarily beautiful. The heavily woven fabric of the dining room gives the

eft: picnic at Rosendals. **Above:** Waldemarsudde
Right: the magnificent interior of Rosendals Slott

impression of being in a tent. Tiled stoves are abundant, as are assorted artefacts and other fine details. In front of the palace is a large bowl made in porphyry from the king's own workshops at Älvdalen in the centre of the country. The bowl was carved from a single stone block and brought to Stockholm in 1825 by 170 men, accompanied by fiddlers.

As you leave Rosendals Slott, continue east on Rosendalsvägen to Rosendals Wärdhus – an inn built in 1915 and open for lunch during the summer months – and then to **Rosendals Trägårdar** (Gardens). The latter

is a bio-dynamic market garden that has been managed by a foundation since 1984. Its aim is not just to use bio-dynamic cultivation methods but also to run courses, lectures and exhibitions. There are plants for sale and you can select your own bouquet of flowers from the garden in summer.

The café serves excellent home-made food and is a highly recommended lunch stop. If the weather allows, you can take your meal to the apple grove and enjoy a picnic in the bucolic atmosphere of the trees. Be warned that this is a popular place for Swedes to while away an afternoon so the queues may be long at the garden café.

After you have dined and rested, stroll east for about 500m (⅓ of a mile) on Rosendalsvägen to Djurgårdsbrunnsbron to get bus No 69, which will take you to **Thielska Galleriet** on Sjötullsbacken 6 (Mon–Sat noon–4pm, Sun 1–4pm). If you would rather take the 20-minute walk there, you should head south on Manillavägen and then east on Djurgårdsvägen. The banker Ernest Thiel commissioned architect Ferdinand Boberg (who also designed Waldemarsudde) to design a dignified villa on Djurgården for his large and valuable collection of contemporary paintings. However, during World War I, Thiel lost most of his fortune. In 1924, the state bought his collection, which mostly covers Nordic art from the late 19th and early 20th centuries, and opened Thielska Galleriet in his villa two years later.

The National Romantic Movement

Thiel was a controversial figure in the banking world. In an attempt to counter the influence of the traditionalist Konstkademin (Royal Academy of Arts), Thiel offered substantial support to painters who were members of the artists' union, which was established in 1866. At Thielska there are paintings by all the major Swedish artists who formed an artists' colony at Gréz-sur-Loing, south of Paris. These include Carl Larsson, Bruno Liljefors, Karl Nordström, and August Strindberg (better known as a dramatist), all part of the National Romantic Movement of the late 19th and early 20th centuries. The collection also includes paintings by Eugéne Jansson, Anders Zorn and Prins Eugen, as well as wooden figures by Axel Petersson and sculptures by Christian Eriksson. Thiel also acquired works by leading foreign artists, including some by his good friend Edvard Munch (1863–1944).

Above: see works by Munch in Thielska Galleriet's collection of modern Nordic art

5. DROTTNINGHOLM *(see pull-out map)*

This tour covers Drottningholm's palace, theatre, park and Chinese Pavilion. The buildings and grounds are included on UNESCO's World Heritage list while the royal family uses part of the 17th-century palace as a residence. The splendid baroque park is a beautiful place for walks.

You can drive or take public transport to Drottningholm (T-Brommaplan and bus Nos 177, 300, 323), but the approach from the water (May–Sept from Stadshusbron) is unbeatable. If you visit in the summer, you might want to pack a picnic. Plan to spend most of the day on this itinerary.

Drottningholms Slott (May–Aug: daily 10am–4.30pm; Sept: daily noon–3.30pm; Oct–Apr: Sat, Sun noon–3.30pm) was inspired by the architecture of French chateaux. Indeed it has often been compared to Versailles, albeit on a somewhat smaller scale. Its present appearance emerged towards the end of the 17th century, when it was considered to be one of the most lavish buildings of the age. Tessin the Elder (1615–81), who found his inspiration primarily in Italian architecture, succeeded in creating a building to glorify royal power. The project was completed by Tessin the Younger while leading 17th-century architects such as Carl Hårleman and Jean Eric Rehn finished the interiors.

The interiors, which span the 17th, 18th and 19th centuries, are quite magnificent. One of the most beautiful rooms, Queen Hedvig Eleonora's State Bedroom, features

Above: the Drottningholms Slottsteater
Right: on the boat to Drottningholm

a richly ornamented baroque style designed by Tessin the Elder. Sweden's most prominent artists and craftsmen spent 15 years decorating the room, which was eventually completed in 1683. Also impressive is Queen Lovisa Ulrika's Library, designed by Eric Rehn. The vast collection in its splendid setting shows the deeply significant impact as a patroness the queen had on art and science in 18th-century Sweden.

When you walk into the Upper South Bodyguard Room, the anteroom to the State Room, you'll probably want to look up at the gorgeous ceiling paintings by Johan Sylvius and stucco works by Giovanni and Carlo Carove. The anteroom is still used for ceremonial occasions. Sylvius also created the trompe l'oeil paintings on the walls of the staircase, which give the impression that the spacious interior extends even further into the palace. The writing table by George Haupt in the Queen's Room is an excellent example of the exquisite craftsmanship on display.

Gustav III's Golden Age

As you leave the palace, you will come to the **Drottningholms Slottsteater** (May: noon–4.30pm; Jun–Aug: 11am–4.30pm; Sept: 1–3.30pm), which is undoubtedly the greatest treasure of the island. The theatre opened in 1766 to honour Queen Louisa Ulrika, the mother of Gustav III. Gustav's two great loves were theatre and French culture – he could write French far better than he wrote Swedish – and it is said that he would have much preferred to be an actor or a playwright than a king. Gustav III was, however, also a patriot who was determined to transform the country's tradition of French theatre into a Swedish one. Thus he replaced the French thespians from Drottningholm with Swedes in pursuit of his ambition to encourage a Golden Age of the native arts.

But for all his enthusiasm for culture, Gustav's benevolent despotism was not popular with his unruly nobility. His assassination in 1792 at a masked ball at Kungliga Operan (the Royal Opera) inspired Verdi's *Un Ballo in Maschera*, a memorial of which Gustav himself might have approved. On his death, the Slottsteater fell into disuse.

It was not until the 1920s that the building was used again, after Professor Agne Beijer discovered it, complete and undamaged, just waiting for restoration. Today its original backdrops and stage machinery are the oldest still used anywhere in the world. Attend a drama here on a warm summer evening and you will feel as if you have been transported in time.

The grassy expanse behind Slottsteater that borders the lake is a popular picnic spot. As the Canada geese edge ever closer to snatch bread crumbs, and children run barefoot across the lawn, it's possible to imagine the leisurely life that generations of royalty have enjoyed at Drottningholm. If you don't really fancy a picnic, Drottningholms Värdshus, just a few hundred metres from the entrance to the palace, is good for lunch. As you stroll through the baroque park behind the palace, which gives fine views of this architectural gem, you'll notice on one of the parterres a bronze statue of Hercules (1680s) by the Dutch Renaissance sculptor Adrian de Vries.

Chinese Transplant

Heading southwest from the gardens, you will soon see the **Kina Slott** (Chinese Pavilion; daily May–Aug: 11am–4.30pm; Sept: noon–3.30pm). The pavilion, a 33rd birthday present to Queen Lovisa Ulrika from her husband, King Adolf Fredrik, was made in Stockholm, shipped to Drottningholm, and assembled just a few hundred metres behind the palace. After about a decade, it was taken down and replaced. The polished tile building was designed by Carl Fredrik Adelcrantz, who also designed the Slottsteater. The Kina Slott is typical of its era, when there was considerable European interest in China, after the newly formed East India Company made its first journey there in 1733. Interest waned after the queen's death in 1782, but emerged once again in the 1840s.

The Kina Slott is an example of what was thought to be typical Chinese style, made more authentic by artefacts from China and Japan. Great efforts have been made to restore the interior to its original state. At the end of the 18th century, Gustav III's courtiers would sun themselves in the pavilion's gardens. Less fortunate were the silkworms introduced to Kanton, the adjacent small village, by a court eager to produce cheap silk. The worms were no match for Swedish winters. Alongside is the Confidencen Pavilion, where the king could take his meals undisturbed. The Turkish-style 'watch tent', built as a barracks for Gustav III's dragoons, houses an estate museum.

Left and Above: inside the restored Chinese Pavilion

6. SÖDERMALM *(see map, p41)*

This walking tour takes in fine city views and old workers' cottages along Åsöberget. The neighbourhood is full of artists' studios and galleries, and features the casual chic of restaurants around Nytorget.

To start this itinerary at Katarinahissen in Stadsgården, take the subway to T-Slussen or bus Nos 3, 43, 46, 53, 55, 59 or 76 to Slussen.

The Södermalm area, generally known as 'Söder' (South), is the city's largest neighbourhood, with 90,000 residents. Yet it retains the air of a small town, with its own character and dialect. Söder rises sharply from the water on slopes lined with old wooden cottages with some of the best views of the city. There are plenty of hilly parks and allotments in the built-up areas, and numerous shops, bars and restaurants. Indeed Söder has more restaurants than any other part of Stockholm. The lively nightlife has none of the air of superiority you might find in the more fashionable district of Östermalm.

Söder's residents are welcoming and down-to-earth, in keeping with the area's history as a workers' quarter. Unlike much of the city, Södermalm wasn't razed in the first half of the 20th century. It was in one of the more humble parts of Söder that Greta Garbo was born in 1905. By the 1920s politicians recognised the historical importance of the *söderkåkar* (cottages), which they protected by law.

Södermalm is huge, so this itinerary is selective, but it takes in some key sights while providing a glimpse into the soul of Söder. Start at **Katarinahissen** (Mon–Sat 7.30am–10pm, Sun 10am–10pm), which

Above: historic homes, Åsögatan
Left: Katarina Kyrka

is a 38-m (125-ft) lift opened to the public in 1883 and still a prominent silhouette on the skyline. Sweden's first neon sign, advertising Stomatol toothpaste, was erected here. Since the 1930s the sign has shone from a nearby rooftop. The original steam-operated lift switched to electricity in 1915, and in the 1930s was replaced by a new model. Some 500,000 passengers a year enjoy the spectacular view of the city from the top of the lift.

From Katarinahissen, walk straight ahead to **Mosebacke Torg** with its attractive square, featuring Nils Sjögren's sculpture *The Sisters*. The Mosebacke area got its name from a miller and landowner, Moses Israelsson, the son-in-law of Johan Hansson Hök, who operated two mills on the hilltop plateau in the 17th century. Mosebacke became a centre for entertainment. A theatre built in 1852 was later destroyed by fire and then replaced in 1859 by Södra Teatern, designed by Johan Frederik Åbom. Go through the gateway leading to Mosebake Terrass and enjoy another splendid view of the city.

Hell's Forecourt

Head east on Fiskargatan and stop at No 12's experimental fireproof gable design, *Morning Light,* an *al secco* painting on limestone plaster. From Fiskargatan, turn right onto Svartensgatan in the Häckejäll (Hell's Forecourt) district. In the 17th century people believed that witches gathered here on the cliffs before flying to Blåkulla, where the devil held court. Witches and trolls were in the habit of kidnapping children and carrying them off to Blåkulla. The witchcraft trials of 1675–6 led to the loss of many innocent lives, including children who were sentenced to die for bearing false witness. The witch saga continues as you head down Katarinakyrkobacke to **Katarina Kyrka**, where prayers were uttered against the witches. At Roddargatan next to the church there still stands an area of old wooden houses inhabited by the city's most destitute people. In this densely populated area, with its taverns and frequent arguments and fights, rumours spread easily.

Refuge was often sought in the church. The buildings on Katarinaberget date partly from the 18th century, but churches have been built here since the early 14th century. Earlier chapels were replaced in 1656 with the more impressive Katarina Kyrka, designed by Jean de la Vallée. King Karl X Gustav oversaw the building of the church and insisted that it should have a central nave with the pulpit in the centre. In 1723 the church was badly damaged by fire but was restored over

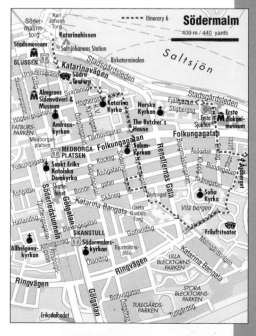

the next two decades. A new copper roof was added in 1988. Two years later, on the night of 16 May 1990, another fire destroyed the church, apart from the outer walls. Ove Hildemark designed a restoration, to which end the architects used 17th-century building methods. The central dome was joined with heavy timbering in the traditional way and the collapsed central arch was rebuilt with specially made bricks in 17th-century style. In 1995 the church was consecrated and many considered it more beautiful than ever. Public donations paid for much of the SEK 270 million work.

Head west on Högbergsgatan and take a peek at Nytorgsgatan 5, one of the more beautiful red *söderkåkar*, then walk south on Nytorgsgatan. You will cross Mäster Mikaelsgata, named after Mikael Reisurer, who was the city's executioner 1635–50. When you come to Tjärhovsgatan, cross the street and check out the pink **Butcher's House** building at 36–8. It was built at the end of the 18th century and generations of butchers worked here until the municipality bought the building in the 1920s. In 1841 the building was remodelled and given its present appearance. The little summer house in the courtyard provided a quiet refuge for authors Oscar Levertin and Ludvig Nordström. The garden is being restored to its late 19th-century glory.

The Bohemian Quarter

Continue south on Nytorgsgatan and turn right on Bondegatan to Söder-mannagatan. Here, in the city's bohemian quarter, with its galleries, artists and traditional craftspeople, are sundry workshops. Svart Kaffe is a typical, unpretentious Söder coffee shop, with a clientele often dressed in black T-shirts and jeans. Head east on Skånegatan, where there are more galleries, artists' shops, second-hand and antique stores and funky boutiques, till you reach **Nytorget**. This square is perhaps the city's most pleasant, with outdoor cafés in a row on the sunny side. At Nytorgsgatan 38 is Café String, whose interior furnishings are for sale. Next door is Klara, an interior decorating shop that sells the latest in Scandinavian design. The park at Nytorget is often full of families and couples, or solitary newspaper readers with a cup of latté at

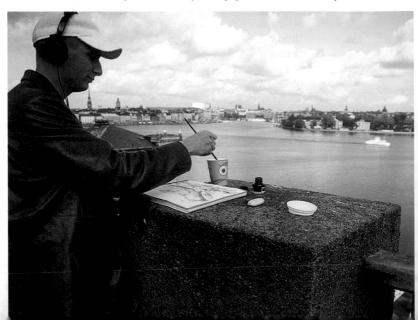

their side. Stop for lunch at Tevere, Nytorgsgatan 89, considered by many to have the city's best pizza. Just a few doors up the street is A H's Glas Bar, where you can enjoy a home-made ice cream.

Walk south on Malmgårdsvägen, which features a 300-year-old Werner Groen Malmgård (Suburban Mansion). Stop at Vita Bergen's Handels Trädgård (Wed–Fri 11am–3pm), Stockholm's oldest market garden (1664). Turn up Lilla Mejtens Gränd to enter **Vita Bergen** (White Mountain), a park known for the Swedish TV show that broadcasts from its open-air theatre. As you stroll north through the park to Mäster Pers Gränd and Bergsprangsgränd, you'll find houses built in the 18th century for harbour and factory workers. In 1736 the building of new houses was prohibited due to the risk of fire, but the slum districts were exempted. So areas like this still have houses with their original character.

Sofia Kyrka was built early in the 20th century, and the area became a leafy hillside park. To the east is an area of cottages with allotment gardens typical of Söder. Head north out of the park on Stora Mejtens Gränd to Ploggatan, crossing Skånegatan and then Bondegatan to **Åsögatan** and **Åsöberget**. Early 18th-century wooden cottages for port workers on Sågargatan and Lotsgatan are plentiful here; Åsöberget offers fine views of the water and city.

Head west and turn north at Erstagatan, crossing the busy Folkungagatan and then past Ersta Sjukhus (Hospital) to **Fjällgatan**. This street inspired Söder's best-known writer, Per Anders Fogelström (1917–98), to write: 'Fjällgatan must be the city's most beautiful street. It's an old-fashioned narrow street which runs along the hilltop with well-maintained cobble-stones… and with street lights jutting out from the houses. Then the street opens up and gives a fantastic view of the city and the water…'

The Last Penny

Fjällgatan is a stop on the city's bus-tour routes so you might have to jostle for space as you gaze at the view. Many of the houses were built along this picturesque street after a devastating fire in 1723. Mamsell Josabeth's Steps were named after the artist Josabeth Sjöbert (1812–82). Sista Styverns Trappor is an alley of steps once known as Mikaelsgränd after a 17th-century executioner. It was renamed after the inn, Sista Styvern (The Last Penny).

Fjällgatan has a café offering cold drinks, coffee and ice cream but if you fancy something more substantial, Hermann's is well worth visiting. While it is a vegetarian restaurant, its generous home-made buffet lunches and pastries are bound to satisfy non-vegetarians as well. Sit in the glass-topped veranda with its fantastic view and your meal will taste even better.

Left: capturing the scene from Fjällgatan, 'the city's most beautiful street'
Above: child's play at Nytorget square

7. ÖSTERMALM *(see map, p45)*

This afternoon expedition takes in the concealed jewel of a museum, Hallwylska Museet (Hallwyl Museum), and the magnificent Gold Room of the Historiska Museet as well as a stroll along elegant Strändvägen.

To get to Hallwylska Museet at Hamngatan 4, you should take the subway to T-Östermalm or bus Nos 46, 47, 55, 62, 69 or 76. The museum can be visited only with a guide; there are frequent English-language tours in the middle of summer, but during the rest of the year, English-language tours take place only on Sun at 1pm.

Countess Wilhelmina von Hallwyl was considered more than a little strange by her contemporaries but today we should be grateful for her penchant for collecting objects both rare and commonplace, all culled from a lifetime's travels.

It is as a happy result of the countess's obsession that we now have **Hallwylska Museet** (Tues–Fri 11.45am–4pm, Sat–Sun 11.30am –4pm; English language tours daily at 1pm). The countess's former residence is now the home of nearly 70,000 objects, including her furniture and personal knick knacks, all of which she lovingly collected and meticulously catalogued. The results of her passion for collecting, which originated in her childhood, covered the whole field of the world's cultural history.

She decided at a young age to transform her home into a museum, to which end she gathered a diverse range of objects over more than 70 years, in the course of journeys through Europe, Africa and the Orient. She wanted to illustrate bygone as well as contemporary forms of living, from magnificent examples of sculpture and art to the homely toothbrush and moustache twirler displayed on the bedroom dresser. The collection varies in quality, it never lacks in fascination.

It Must Be Perfect

The impressive facade at Hamngatan 4 leads into a courtyard flanked by two wings and a pair of secondary buildings, the latter being joined by a decorative central edifice that serves as a backdrop. A gateway through the middle of the main building links the courtyard to the street. The entire composition is a model of symmetry. Here popular cabaret performances in Swedish are held in the courtyard in summer.

The beauty of the facade is nothing, however, compared with the treasures

Above: a few of the 70,000 objects on display in Hallwylska Museet

that you will find behind the heavy gates. Built in 1892–97 as a residence for the incredibly wealthy Countess and Count von Hallwyl, these sumptuous rooms are fit for royalty. The von Hallwyls spared no expense in designing and building their Stockholm residence. The architect Isak Gustav Clason, much in vogue with the rich and powerful at the time (he also takes the credit for designing the Nordic Museum, among other projects), was commissioned to carry out the work, assisted by the decorative painter and artistic adviser Julian Kronberg. The countess was adamant that everything should be perfect, right down to the final little detail. Her pefectionism is plainly evident in the billiards room, which features gilt-leather wallpaper and walnut panelling. On the subject of superior-quality craftsmanship, check out the billiard balls sculpted into the marble fireplace.

The Countess's Moustache

The paintings in the gallery, mostly 16th- and 17th-century Flemish, were purchased over a period of just two years which, given their sheer number, is quite astonishing. Adjoining the gallery is the family bowling alley, now a showcase for top-class glazed earthenware. A rich variety of household objects are also on display in every room, all illustrating the eccentric brilliance of the collector. In contrast with the amount of energy she expended on her passion for preservation, the countess paid scant attention to her own appearance. In a controversial portrait, displayed in the smoking room, she is dressed plainly, with virtually no jewellery, and a small moustache is clearly visible. Although she insisted on electric lighting and hot water for a bathroom that was quite modern for its time, she would bathe more simply – in an old wooden tub with a bucket of water.

To take a tour through the palace is to embark on an expedition that chronicles one illustrious family's fascinating history. Count von Hallwyl

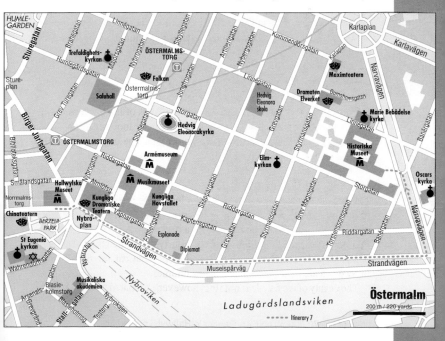

and his wife had four daughters, one of whom died as an infant. The other three, Ellen, Ebba and Irma, are all brought vividly to life by their portraits. The intellectual Ellen was the first woman in the country to earn an academic degree, but she was prohibited from the pursuit of a profession by a prevailing ethos that limited women's involvement in public affairs. Similarly ahead of her time, the passionate artist Ebba caused a family scandal when she divorced her first husband in order to marry her son's art teacher. The vain Irma had a passion for clothes and jewels, baubles that her mother disdained.

An 1896 Steinway

The daughters' biographies resound as you walk through the rooms, each one decorated in the style of a different historical period – as was the fashion at the time. The main salon, in late baroque style, is built around four grandiose Gobelins tapestries and is finished in 24-carat gold leaf. The most remarkable object here is a Steinway grand piano dating from 1896, adapted to fit into its majestic setting with a casing of hardwood and inlaid wood. In 1990 it was flown to New York in two sections, weighing a total of 900kg (1,980lb) for a renovation that lasted several months. Sometimes concerts are performed on this magnificent piano, the focal point of the lavish dinners and dances that the countess was reluctantly obliged to hold a few times each year.

Leaving Hallwyska Palatset, head east on Hamngatan for about 50 metres (165ft) to the magnificent Jugendstil **Kungliga Dramatiska Teatern** (Royal Dramatic Theatre), designed by Fredrik Lilljekvist and opened in 1908. The facade, inspired by the Viennese architectural style, is in white marble. Christian Eriksson provided the masterful relief frieze, Carl Milles the centre section, and John Börjesson the bronze statues. These are complemented in the foyer by Börjesson's *Tragedy* and Theodor Lundberg's *Comedy*. The lavish design continues inside; if you happen to follow this itinerary on a Saturday, there is a guided tour at 3pm, in English on special request by groups.

Above and Right: exhibits at the Historiska Museet's Gold Room

Worth seeing in particular is the ceiling in the foyer by Carl Larsson. Ingmar Bergman still regularly directs plays here; but all productions are in Swedish. You can still soak up the grand atmosphere and splendid view by stopping for coffee at Café Pauli on the Dramaten's balcony. Artist Georg Pauli gave his name to the café, which displays his paintings.

An Elegant Boulevard

As you leave Dramaten, cross Hamngatan to the harbour and head east along **Strandvägen**. The palatial houses along Strandvägen were built in the early 20th century by Stockholm's 10 richest citizens, seven of whom were wholesale merchants. This was a hilly, muddy harbour area until a campaign began in advance of the 1897 Stockholm Exhibition to create a grand avenue unrivalled in Europe. This was a long process, as the old wooden quay erected in the 1860s was still a bit of an eyesore. Up until the 1940s boats would bring firewood from the archipelago islands to the quay. Eventually, Strandvägen, with its three rows of lime trees, became the elegant boulevard that had been envisioned. It is still a popular place to wander. As you walk, you'll notice some of the old wooden sailing vessels anchored along the quay, rescued by boat enthusiasts who have lovingly refurbished them. Beside every boat is a sign describing its history.

At the corner of Strandvägen and Narvavägen, turn left, heading north on Narvavägen to the **Historiska Museet** (Musuem of National Antiquities) with its spectacular Gold Room (Tues–Sun 11am–5pm, Thur 11am–8pm). The museum, designed by Bengt Romare and Georg Sherman, opened in 1943. Bror Marklund designed the decoration around the entrance and the richly detailed bronze gateways. The museum has a prominent collection from the Viking era as well as from the early Middle Ages. But without doubt the most amazing sight is the Guldrummet (Gold Room), where many of Historiska Museet's gold treasures were gathered in the early 1990s for a breathtaking display. This 700-sq m (7,535-sq ft) underground vault was built with 250 tons of reinforced concrete to ensure security. The room is divided into two circular sections. The inner section houses the main collection, with 50kg (110lb) of gold treasures and 250kg (550lb) of silver from the Bronze Age to the Middle Ages.

These amazing exhibits come from some unedxpected sources. For instance the gold collars were found between 1827 and 1864 in a stone quarry in eastern Sweden, in a ditch on the island of Öland, and on a spike in a barn. Note, too, the Elisabeth reliquary, originally a drinking goblet mounted with gold and precious stones in the 11th century. In about 1230, a silver cover was added to enclose the skull of St Elisabeth. In 1631, during the Thirty Years War, it was seized as a trophy for Sweden.

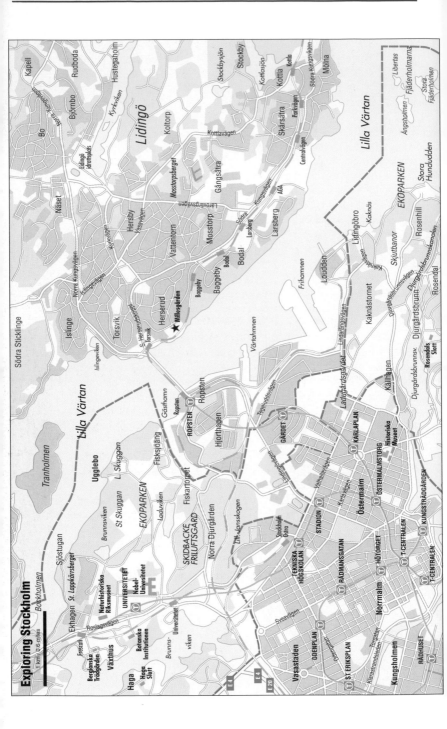

8. MILLESGÅRDEN *(see map, p40)*

This tour visits the island of Lidingö, where Carl Milles, one of Sweden's foremost sculptors, built a residence and studio, complete with a series of terraces, gardens and towering sculptures, in 1908.

To get to Millesgården at Herserudsvägen 30, Lidingö, take the subway to T-Ropsten, then bus No 203 or train to Torsvik.

Carl Milles (1875–1955) was one of the 20th century's most eminent sculptors. From 1931 to 1951 he lived in the United States, where he became famous for monumental sculptures such as the *Meeting of the Rivers* in St Louis and the *Resurrection* fountain in the National Memorial Park outside Washington DC. Fifteen of his public works can be seen in Stockholm, including the *Orpheus* fountain in front of Konserthuset at Hörtorget.

In 1906 he bought land on the island of Lidingö to build a house, designed by Karl Magnus Bengtson, which was completed in 1908. Milles lived here with his wife until 1931 and again after his return from the US. Ultimately they donated the property to the Swedish people. Here, summer after summer, Milles reproduced the statues that made him more famous in America than in Sweden. Milles's works seem to defy gravity. They soar, fly and step lightly over water, emphasised by their position on cliff terraces.

Millesgården features a veritable cascade of architectural impressions from different periods and places. The entry portal and two of the colonnades were rescued when Gustav Adolfs Torg's Hotel Rydberg and the former opera house were torn down. The house covers a total of 18,000 sq m (193,750 sq ft) and includes Milles' studios with originals and replicas of his work. It has a beautiful garden, which is a work of art in its own right, and a fine view over the water.

In the late 1940s Milles' half-brother, Evert Milles, designed the low bungalow-type building on the lower terrace. This is *Annes hus*, the house of Milles' assistant, Anne Hedmark, whose interior design

Above: the Millesgården garden is itself a work of art
Right: a Milles sculpture reaches for the sky

– by Josef Frank – is still intact. Carl and his wife Olga spent their summers here after their return to Europe in 1951 and it was here in the music room that Milles died in 1955.

Milles wrote in 1949: 'I want Anne to live in a new low house on the Lower Terrace. I want Anne to live there even after I have died, it shall be the most beautiful, airiest house with a marvelous view, where she can play music, enjoy life, entertain her friends, write letters, sew, and have spiritual relaxation.' A walk through the house confirms that Milles's wishes were indeed granted. Anne lived here until 1986 and then the house was used for occasional guests or official visits until it was opened to the public in 1991, supported by a private foundation.

A sculpture hall for temporary exhibitions, designed by Johan Celsing Arkitektkontor, opened in 1999. Its three galleries are housed under a single roof, but the floor levels vary, allowing an exhibit to be viewed from different vantage points. Also in 1999, a garden in the style and spirit of pioneer landscape designer Emma Lundberg opened.

9. FJÄDERHOLMARNA *(see map, p48)*

This tour brings the archipelago to the city's doorstep, just a 25-minute boat ride away. Rich in history dating back to the 1600s, the island was restored in the mid-1980s and now has an attractive harbour, restaurants, museums, handicraft shops and art galleries.

To get to Fjäderholmarna, take the boat from Nybrokajen or Slusssen (May–Sept). The boats leave every half hour from Nybrokajen.

Fjäderholmarna, part of Ekoparken, the National City Park, has always been a popular destination for Stockholmers as it is the closest archipelago island to the centre of town. But while today's visitors head for the cliffs to sun themselves or to the restaurants to dine on fresh seafood, in the 1600s fishermen stopped here for one thing only: a glass of *snaps,* Swedish spiced vodka.

Stora Fjäderholmen, the largest of the group of three small islands, was the last place at which fishermen could stop for a drink before they came into town with their goods. It was also the first tavern on the journey home, which was not necessarily a good thing, especially for wives looking forward to the return of sober husbands. Snaps was also sold at the tavern on Stora Fjäderholmen for less than the usual price by the 'snaps king', L O Smith. The tavern became very popular and an outlook tower with a restaurant was added, but the tower was torn down in the 1940s and the tavern was closed during World War II when the area was taken over by the military and landing was forbidden. Access to the public was restored in the mid-1980s and some 200,000 people now visit the island every year.

Above: a Millesgården landmark
Right: Fjäderholmarna's pier restaurant

The old tavern is now Fjäderholmarnas Krog, an inn that serves great food, especially seafood. A restaurant at the pier specialises in the likes of smoked salmon and smoked mackerel that you can can eat at outdoor tables in the sea breeze. Check out the ice cream parlour for a satisfying dessert.

Exploring the Island

An exploration of the island should stimulate your appetite. Sights include beautifully maintained old boats in a museum devoted to traditional and recreational boating, crafts workshops, a playground, a Baltic aquarium (with an adjoining museum) and an outdoor theatre that stages children's shows in summer. You could join a walking tour of the island, hourly between 11.30am and 2.30pm in summer. If you ask, the guide should speak in English as well as Swedish. You might learn about the pirate Nils Emil who inhabited the smaller Liberty Island for 30 years, until 1940. No one quite knows how he managed to survive the cold Baltic winters but he made himself useful to the authorities by checking the thickness of the ice. The island was also a favourite retreat of the soprano Jenny Lind, who liked to spend summer afternoons under a huge oak tree dating back hundreds of years.

Literally, 'Fjäderholmarna' means 'The Feather Islands', but the name has nothing to do with feathers, despite the multitude of seabirds – it comes from the Swedish word *fjärdern,* which means 'bay'. Sweden's last remaining gas-powered lighthouse is on Liberty Island, but the third island, Ängsholmen, has a less illuminating claim to fame – it served as the dumping site for the city's latrines in the late 19th century. Now the island, which is owned by the king, has regained its natural beauty and the residents of its few houses live there by royal permission.

The handicraft shops on Stora Fjäderholmen are good places at which to find souvenirs. Island handicrafts include metalwork, weaving, textile printing, woodcarving, pottery and glass making. There is also an art gallery. The first Swedish malt whisky distillery, Mackmyra, has an outpost here and welcomes group tastings (tel: 08-55 60 15 60). Before you board the boat back, you could take a dip in the refreshingly cool waters of the Baltic. The sample taste of the archipelago that Fjäderholmarna offers will no doubt be so enticing that you will want to return one day.

city itineraries

10. EKOPARKEN *(see map, p53)*

The world's first national city park, Ekoparken (Eco Park) is a huge set of green lungs stretching in a 12-km (7-mile) arch from Ulriksdal Slott in the north to Fjäderholmarna in the south. The best way to explore it in summer is on the inexpensive, one-hour 'Around Brunnsviken' boat tour. There's an English-speaking guide on the last tour every day.

To join the 3pm English-language tour of the 'Around Brunnsviken' boat trips (mid-June–mid-Aug), take bus No 515 from Odenplan to Haga Forum. If you would like to visit Ekoparken at other times of the year, the information centre at Haga Forum is a natural entry point. To get to Ekoparken, you

can take bus No 40 from Odenplan or the subway to T-Universitet to explore three other interesting sights in the park – Stora Skuggan, Bergianska Trädgården and the Naturhistoriska Riksmuseet. To reach Ulriksdals Slott in the north of the park, take bus No 503.

The feature that distinguishes **Ekoparken** from other European city parks is its wildness. Large tracts of historical parklands and untamed wilderness intersect throughout this vast green space. The park provides a quite brilliant splash of life-giving space and colour in the city's mass of brick and concrete. Futhermore, in addition to its architectural jewels and fascinating history, the park is also a refuge for all types of rare plants, insects, birds, fish and animals. The Isblads marsh area, located in the southeastern section of the park, is a popular bird-watching site. The oak trees in the park are hundreds of years old and shelter rare butterflies and beetles.

Large parts of Ekoparken are spread around the Brunnsviken inlet, which makes the boat tour perfect for an introduction to sights you might want to explore more thoroughly later. The first stop is **Bergianska Trädgården** (Botanical Gardens), established in 1790 and featuring more than 9,000 types of plants in beautiful natural settings. **Naturhistoriska Riksmuseet** (Swedish Museum of Natural History), one of the 10 largest museums of its kind in the world, was founded in 1730 by the botanist Carl von Linné as part of the Academy of Sciences. There are some 17 million exhibits. Since the museum was modernised in the 1990s, with the aim of providing more 'experience-based knowledge', the **Cosmonova**, which features both a planetarium and an IMAX cinema, has become one of its biggest attractions.

The King's Childhood Home

The boat eventually wends its way past **Haga Slott**, one of the numerous treasures of Haga Park. In the mid-18th century King Gustav III decided to create a royal park in the popular Haga area of the city and the architect Fredrik Magnus Piper created an English-style park with some unusual buildings. A royal palace inspired by Versailles in France was also planned

Above: Haga Park's Ekotemplet dates back to the 18th century

but construction was halted after the king's death. You can see the foundation of the building, which is fascinating in itself. Haga Slott was built in 1802–4 for Gustav IV Adolf, and it was the childhood home of the present king, Carl XVI Gustav and his sisters. Now it is used for government receptions.

Haga Park is best enjoyed via a stroll down its serpentine paths, which lead you to one architectural surprise after another. Among them are the **Koppartälten**'s bright blue and gold Roman-style battle tents, designed by Louis Jean Desprez and completed in 1790. Once used as stables and for accommodation, they now house a restaurant, café and museum (June–Aug: Tues–Sun 11am–5pm; Sept–May: Tues–Fri 11am–3pm, Sat–Sun 11am–5pm).

The lawn stretching down from Koppartälten to Brunnsviken is called Stora Pelousen, and is a popular spot for sunbathing and picnics in the summer, and for skiing and sledging in winter. Just at the rear of the lawn is **Gustav III's Pavilion** (May–Aug: Tue–Sun hourly guided tours 11am–3pm), a Gustavian masterpiece designed by Olof Tempelman, with Louis Masreliéz as the interior designer.

Ekotemplet, just beyond Gustav III's Pavilion, also designed by Louis Jean Desprez in the 1790s, served as a royal dining room in the summer. The 18th century's fascination with anything Chinese led to the construction of the **Kinesiska Pagoden** (Chinese Pagoda). By contrast, the park's newest attraction is the **Fjärils &**

Above: a lawn game outside Haga Park's Roman-style battle tent

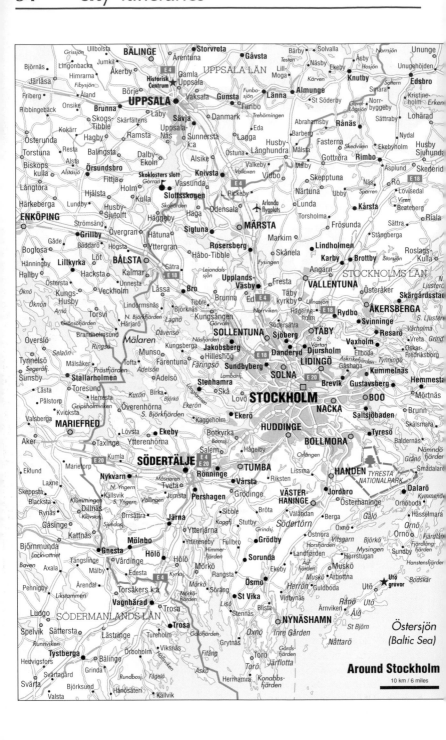

Around Stockholm

10 km / 6 miles

Östersjön
(Baltic Sea)

Fågelhuset (Bird and Butterfly House), where hundreds of exotic butterflies and birds fly freely around greenhouses in a humid tropical rainforest environment (Apr–Sept: Tues–Fri 10am–4pm, Sat, Sun 11am–5:30pm; Oct–Mar: Tues–Fri 10am–3pm, Sat–Sun 11am–4pm).

If you want to venture as far as Ekoparken's most northerly treasure, **Ulriksdals Slott** (June–Aug: Tue–Sun hourly guided tours noon–3pm), you can take the bus, and you won't be disappointed. The palace sits on a headland in lush surroundings in the bay of Edsviken. At the entrance is one of the city's best-known restaurants, which does an excellent smorgasbord, known as Ulriksdals Wärdhus. The original palace, built in the 1640s, was bought by Dowager Queen Hedvig Eleonora in 1669. In later years it was donated to her grandson, Ulrik, after whom it was renamed Ulriksdal. It acquired its baroque exterior in the 18th century. You might want to visit the living room of Gustav VI Adolf in the rebuilt Knights Hall, which contains furniture by the great architect and designer Carl Malmsten.

The park has 300-year-old lime trees and two sculptures by Carl Milles near the pool in front of the palace. There is more artwork and sculpture displayed in the Orangery, which was designed by Tessin the Elder in the 1660s. A riding school was converted into a theatre, Confidencen, in the 1750s, and performances are staged there every summer.

11. BIRKA *(see map, p54)*

Birka is a journey back in time to the days of the Vikings. Extensive archaeological discoveries on this island in Lake Mälaren reveal a lot about life in the 8th century. The finds are displayed in a new museum.

To get to Birka in summer (1 May–26 Sept), take an hour and 45-minute boat trip from Stadhusbron. A guided tour of old Birka takes 1 hour 15 minutes. The trail is 1.5 km (1 mile) long and the path is hilly in places. If you want to explore on your own, be sure to follow the numbered signposts. Get an English-language guidebook from the museum. There is a restaurant on the island but this is an ideal spot for a picnic, and a swim.

In June 793, the peaceful prosperity of 8th-century Europe was shattered by the arrival of a new menace from the sea. The image of the bloodthirsty Viking plundering all in his path is one that was to haunt Europe for the next 300 years. More recently however, archaeological finds have forced us to realise that the popular image of the Viking barbarian is nothing more than a myth. Of particular interest to historians are the discoveries at Birka – Sweden's first Viking town – on the island of Björkö west of Stockholm. A

Right: evidence of Birka's rich trading past

millennium after the Viking era, Birka has risen again, this time as part of Sweden's cultural landscape, with its own museum and a place on UNESCO's list of World Heritage sites.

Birka was founded in the mid-8th century and, for nearly 200 years, it flourished as Europe's northernmost mercantile centre. In its heyday it had about 700 inhabitants. No one knows why Birka was abandoned but the growth of trading towns such as Sigtuna is thought to be behind its demise. The discoveries at Birka are evidence of the elaborate trading networks of the Viking age. They portray a society of traders, merchants and skilled craftsmen. The coins, silks, beads, pottery, glass and jewellery found in 3,000 graves around the town reveal links that reached the Byzantine Empire and China.

The town was planned with remarkable simplicity. People lived in modest longhouses that stood in rows overlooking the jetties where ships were moored. These were the vessels in which the Vikings, the warriors of King Svea, sailed on their marauding expeditions. The year 830 was a pivotal one in Scandinavian history. It was then that a monk named Ansgar came to Birka, bringing with him the Christian faith. Until then Sweden had been one of the last outposts of paganism in Europe. Missionaries feared the Vikings, while in Birka the people attributed their success to their pagan gods and saw no reason to renounce them.

A Spiritual Battleground

Ansgar's arrival transformed Birka into a spiritual battleground. Ansgar was a man of burning faith, whose tireless efforts to introduce Christianity to Scandinavia eventually earned him a sainthood. He was actually welcomed in Birka, probably because the people believed it would help to promote trade with Christian lands. But Christianity would not defeat the pagan gods for another 250 years, when the Viking age came to an end as a result of its refusal to tolerate rival divinities. On the crest of the hill fort on Birka stands the Ansgar cross, erected in 1834 to mark 1,000 years since the arrival of Ansgar and Christianity at Birka. From

Top and Above: exhibits and artefacts at the museum illustrate Birka's Viking history
Right: Vaxholm is a picture of tranquillity

here, across the skerry to the north, you can see Adelsö church and the Viking-age royal court, Hovgården.

Archaeologists who work at Birka bring its fascinating history alive through animated and knowledgeable guided tours. It's also a good idea to visit the excellent museum when you first arrive, if you have time, so that your imagination is working even before you begin the tour. The museum complements the archaeological finds in showing how Birka would have looked in its heyday. For anyone who has ever harboured a desire to be an archaeologist, the opportunity to see freshly dug artefacts from excavations in progress is part of what makes a day on Birka such an unusual experience.

12. VAXHOLM *(see map, p54)*

Visit the archipelago's main centre, a strategic point for ships since the 19th century. Take a delightful boat trip and explore the town's roots.

Take a boat (they leave frequently in summer from Strömkajen or Nybrokajen) or bus No 670 from Tekniska Högskolan. The boat trip takes an hour.

The urban area of Vaxholm is the trading centre for the 60 or so islands in the eastern archipelago. It has been a strategic point for shipping since the 16th century, when the area was first inhabited. In 1548 Gustav Vasa ordered the nearby island of Vaxholmen to be fortified. About 300 years later a new fortress was built there, but it lost its military importance and became a civil prison. Today the **Kastellet** citadel features a fortress museum (June: daily noon–4pm; July–Aug: daily 11am–5pm; early Sept: Sat–Sun 11am–5pm; rest of year: by appointment, groups only; tel: 08-541 721 57). There is also a conference section (tel: 08-541 333 61) and bed and breakfast (tel: 08-541 751 10).

Vaxholm retains numerous elements of life in the mid-18th century, when the wealthier Stockholmers began to turn it into an ideal resort and build elegantly decorated wooden summer homes. The wooden buildings with their souvenir shops around the square and along Hamngatan make for a pleasant stroll. Start on Strandvägen, heading away from the harbour, passing the **Vaxholms Hotel**. Traces of the Jugendstil ornamentation are still visible in this elegant hotel designed in 1889 by Erik Lallerstedt. With its beau-

tiful view of the busy harbour, the hotel is a pleasant place at which to eat – herring is a speciality – or have coffee. There are a number of other recommended spots for lunch, including Magasinet on Fiskargatan, which has a terrace that

looks over the fortress. Magasinet is both a restaurant and a shop specialising in Scandinavian interior design and furniture. Two fine restaurants overlooking Västerhamn, the western harbour, are Hamnkrogen and Portobello, a charming Italian restaurant at Södra Hamngatan 6

On leaving the hotel, head north and you will pass the old **Customs House**. Built in 1736, it is Vaxholm's oldest building and one of its first stone houses. **Gamla Skeppsbrokällaren**, for centuries the site of a popular archipelago inn, is next door; it is now a block of privately owned apartments and is currently being renovated to the original design. Just a little further to the north, at the intersection of Fiskaregatan, you will see **Wirströmska Gårdarna**, houses that were built in 1820 and are now protected as an expression of cultural heritage. Heading northeast towards the fortress you will see **Kronudden**, a large building dating back to 1904, when it served as a fortification administration office. Now the building comprises private homes. A short distance to the north is **Batteriet**, where there used to be a series of cannons around the Vaxholm fortress, until they were removed in 1917.

Homestead Museum

Heading northwest on Fiskaregatan you will come to **Norrhamnen**. This, Vaxholm's original fishing harbour, features houses and cottages from the 19th century. It's well worth stopping at the **Hembygdsgården Museet** (Homestead Museum) in a century-old fishing cottage with a pleasant café (Sept–Apr: Mon–Fri 10am–3pm, Sat–Sun 10am–2pm; Jun–Aug: Mon–Fri 10am–6pm, Sat–Sun 10am–4pm). Walk south a few hundred metres to the **Rådhuset**, the 100-year-old law-courts' building, given its present appearance by Cyrillus Johansson in 1925. In Rådhuset Torg there are several fine boutiques selling textiles, clothing, ceramics, crafts and souvenirs. Heading east on Hamngatan you reach **Lägret**, which in 1878 was the exercise area for the soldiers who manned the fortress. The large cottage on the hill was built as a residence for soldiers in 1909.

You will find **Vaxholms Kyrka** in the corner of the Lägret, opposite Kungsgatan. The present church, built between 1760 and 1803, replaced a wooden affair built in the 17th century. Head south on Parkgatan to **Officersparken**, the 19th-century officers' quarters, now given over to private homes. A lovely place to end the afternoon is Café Gröna Längan on Hamngatan. In the summer, you can take coffee and pastries on the veranda; in winter, sit inside and enjoy a mug of steaming cocoa in a pleasant, cosy atmosphere.

Above: a visiting family enjoys a picnic lunch at Vaxholm
Right: tending the garden of one of Vaxholm's 18th-century summer houses

Excursions

1. UPPSALA *(see map, p54)*

This full-day excursion explores Sweden's ancient capital, Uppsala, the last bastion of paganism and the seat of one of Europe's greatest universities. Here you'll find the country's oldest botanical garden, founded by Olof Rudbeck the Elder in 1655 and redesigned almost a century later by the renowned botanist Carl von Linné. Finally, visit the Stonehenge of Sweden at Gamla Uppsala's eerie Kungshögarna.

To get to Uppsala, take the commuter train (Mälardalen line) from Central Station, which leaves twice hourly. The journey takes 40 minutes. Alternatively, you might consider renting a car. Follow the E4 north and exit at Uppsala. Follow the signs for Centrum, where parking is readily available close to the main sights. To reach Gamla Uppsala, where the Kungshögarna are located, you need to catch bus No 2 or 54 (Sundays) from Stora Torget for the 15-minute journey. If you are travelling by car, simply follow the signs for road 290 and Gamla Uppsala.

Uppsala is an appealing blend of ancient capital and bustling university town on the banks of the River Fyrisån. Steeped in history, the city has much to offer the visitor for a full-day excursion. This excursion starts at **Domkyrkan** (daily 8am–6pm) located at the corner of Biskopsgatan and Akademigatan. Uppsala is an episcopal see and the imposing Domkyrkan is the largest gothic cathedral in Scandinavia. Its vaults, dating from 1435, house the shrine of St Erik, an early king who is the patron saint of Sweden, as well as the graves of other monarchs (including Gustav Vasa and his three wives), bishops, generals, and a philosopher or two. The scientist and theologian Emanuel Swedenborg lies here in a massive granite sarcophagus.

University Museum

Cross the road to Akademigatan 3 to visit the **Gustavianum** (Uppsala University Museum), an ancient, onion-domed edifice that houses a 17th-century anatomical theatre built for the Renaissance genius Olof Rudbeck (late Aug–late Dec: daily 11am–4pm; guided tours in English: Sat, Sun 2pm).

From Gustavianum, walk south to the intersection of Biskopsgatan and then walk westwards for a few minutes until you come to **Universitets-hus** (Uppsala Cathedral Museum and Treasure Chamber, Mon–Fri 8am–4pm), which has one of the world's foremost collections of medieval textiles. More treasures are to be found at **Carolina Redviva Library** (winter: Mon–Fri 9am–8pm; summer: Mon–Fri, Sun

Left: many eminent Swedes are interred at Domkyrkan
Right: exhibit at Uppsala University Museum

9am–8pm), which you reach after a few minutes walk by heading south-east on Övre Slottsgatan to the intersection of Dag Hammarskjöldsväg. The building houses Sweden's oldest university library and is worth visiting for a quick peek at the 6th-century Silver Bible and other medieval manuscripts.

The Queen Abdicates

If you continue walking south you can't miss **Uppsala Slott** (Uppsala Castle; early June–late Aug, English guided tours daily 1pm, 3pm), a typically squat, dominating brick fortress from the days of the Vasa dynasty. The construction of the castle was begun by King Gustav Vasa in the mid-16th century and reached its present form in 1757. It was from this castle's magnificent halls that the imperious Queen Kristina abdicated. Apparently she preferred to live in exile in Rome rather than 'rule a country of barbarians'.

Across the road from Uppsala Slott is the **Botaniska Trädgården** (Botanical Garden, daily May–Sept: 7am–8:30pm; Oct–Apr: 7am–7pm) at Nörbyvägen 2. The garden's oldest part is baroque in style and dates back to the mid-17th century. There are more than 13,000 species and sub-species from all over the world in the garden, which been used for teaching and research for 350 years.

After visiting the garden, walk north on Dag Hammarsjköldsväg to Akademigatan, turning left on Sysslomansgatan where, at No 4, you can enjoy an inexpensive buffet lunch (including vegetarian dishes) at Aplers Krog at Kyrkans Hus. After lunch, continue northwest on Sysslomansgatan, turn right at Skogatan and follow the street as it crosses the River Fyris. At the intersection of Svartbäcksgatan, you will arrive at **Linnéträdgården** (Linnaeus Garden, daily, 1 May–31 Aug: 11am–3pm;

Above: theatre, Uppsala University Museum
Left: the gothic cathedral of Domkyrkan

Sept 9am–7pm; closed 1 Oct–30 Apr). This, Sweden's oldest botanical garden, was established in 1655 by Olof Rudbeck the Elder. The garden has now restored the design of the botanist Carl von Linné, who became involved with it in 1745. Some 1,300 different species are arranged in beds of annuals, perennials, spring blocks and autumn blocks.

Also on Svartbäcksgatan, at No 27, is **Linnémuseet** (Linnaeus Museum; 1 June–15 Sept: Tues–Sun noon–4pm, group tours by arrangement). Von Linné and his family lived here, and today the great man's scientific activities are faithfully re-created in an 18th-century milieu, with a partially restored library, a writing room and a collection of natural history specimens.

Walk southeast on Svartbäcksgatan to Stora torget, where you can catch bus No 2 (or on Sun, No 54) to **Gamla Uppsala**. The buses run frequently, and the trip takes about 15 minutes. Our destination is Groaplan, a 5th-century Yngling dynasty bastion. Three huge grave mounds of kings Aun, Egil and Adils (described in the opening passages of *Beowulf*) dominate the evocative cemeteries surrounding Gamla Uppsalakyrkan (Uppsala parish church). This medieval brick edifice replaced Scandinavia's last heathen temple.

A New History Centre

The **Historisk Centrum** (History Centre, daily, May–Aug: 11am–5pm; Sept–Apr: Wed, Sat–Sun noon–3pm; closed mid Dec–1Jan) opened in spring 2000 and is well worth a visit. The centre focuses on the history, legends and folklore surrounding the Kungshögarna, or grave mounds, which are located just behind the museum. Like Egypt's Pyramids and England's Stonehenge, Sweden's Kungshögarna have proved to be a rich source of knowledge about ancient times. This area was the royal seat of the House of Svea, and the burial site is the most distinguished in the country. The three largest burial mounds date from the era of the Great Migration.

Before the construction of the mounds, the dead were cremated together with a range of items thought to be necessary in the next life. 'The Svea believed that the higher the smoke rose into the air, the higher the status achieved by the deceased in heaven,' according to Snorri Sturluson, a 13th-century historian from Iceland. Armour, jewellery, weapons, textiles, everyday tools and other objects excavated from the sites are beautifully displayed in the museum. You can get an English-language map of the mounds and other ancient burial grounds from the museum. In summer, there are twice-daily guided tours (in English) of the museum's collection, at 11.30am and 2.30pm; at other times there is just one English tour, at 11am.

Above: the Linnaeus Garden is the country's oldest botanical garden

2. MARIEFRED *(see map, p54)*

Take a journey on an old-fashioned steamboat to an idyllic town on Lake Mälaren and its imposing Renaissance castle, Gripsholms Slott, at the water's edge. Visit Sweden's new Centre for Graphic Arts and Printmaking, stroll down quaint cobbled lanes, and return to the city by a combination of vintage steam railway and high-speed train.

From mid-May to mid-September, you can travel by steamship to Mariefred from Stadshusbron, a 3½-hour journey. To return, take the vintage steam railway from Mariefred to Läggesta (a 20-minute journey) and then the express train to Stockholm (30 minutes). Alternatively, you can travel both ways by train, or by car, taking the E20 highway and the exit for Mariefred and Gripsholms Slott. There is free parking for visitors to the castle.

Gripsholms Slott (Gripsholm Castle; mid-May–mid-Sept: Mon–Sun 10am–4pm; mid-Sept–mid-May: Sat, Sun and holidays noon–3pm) was intended to be an appropriate residence for the Renaissance ruler Gustav Vasa. Approaching this splendid castle from the water is the ideal way to appreciate the extent to which Vasa's architects succeeded. Whether you arrive by boat or by land, you should start your expedition with a tour of Gripsholms Slott.

The castle's construction commenced in 1537 under the direction of the master-builder Henrik von Köllen. Gustav Vasa's project was part of a new system of national defences. The large Hall of State shows us Gripsholm at the height of its power. The most famous of the 16th-century apartments is Duke Karl's chamber, one of finest interiors of the period in Sweden.

Home to the Kings' Widows

During the 17th century, Gripsholm was used as a dower house (a widow's property for life) by Queen Maria Eleonora (widow of Gustav II Adolf) and Queen Hedvig Eleonora (widow of Karl X). Hedvig Eleonora made considerable changes and additions, among them the Queen's Wing. The reign of Gustav III in the late 18th century marked a new period of brilliance in the castle's history. It was at this time that the exquisite theatre was fitted out in one of the round Renaissance towers. This is one of the best-preserved 18th-century theatres in Europe. Gustav III's Round Drawing Room, a coun-

terpart to Gustav Vasa's Hall of State, dates from the same period. In the Round Drawing Room you can see portraits of Gustav III and his royal contemporaries.

In the 19th century Gripsholm evoked strong national sentiments and the castle came to be regarded as a national monument. Furniture and art of great historical importance were transferred from the various royal residences to Gripsholm to reinforce its national importance and character. A much-debated restoration of the castle took place at the end of the 19th century. Critics called it an attempt to make the castle seem to be even older than it was.

Portraits of Honour

Gripsholm is a showcase for Swedish interior design from the 16th to the late 19th century. Its unique collection of furniture and decorative arts spans 400 years. The castle is internationally known for its outstanding collection of portraits – the Swedish national collection – featuring prominent people from Gustav Vasa's day to the present. Every year, the Gripsholm Association commissions 'portraits of honour' of eminent Swedes for the collection.

After touring the castle, take a stroll into the quaint town of Mariefred, which received its charter in 1605. The ideal place for lunch is Gripsholms Värdhus & Hotel (Gripsholm Inn & Hotel), built on the site of the former monastery, Pax Mariae (Maria's Peace), which gave the town its name. Gripsholms Värdhus is Sweden's oldest inn and its dining room gives a magnificent view over the castle and lake. The inn's wine cellar has remains from the 15th-century monastery. If you want to splash out, stay at the hotel, each room of which is individually designed with period furniture and decor. For a lighter, cheaper lunch, try the beautiful Gripsholms Slottscafé in Lottenlund, which has a good view of Lake Mälaren.

After lunch, continue walking through Mariefred, where wooden houses, some painted red or yellow, are situated along the cobbled lanes. Be sure to see both the 17th-century church on Klostergatan and the 18th-century **Rådhus** (Law Courts) at Rådhustorget, which houses the tourist information office. There are several speciality shops, galleries, and an excellent antiques shop.

Take the short walk back towards the castle to **Grafikens Hus** (May–Aug: Tue–Sun 11am–5pm; Sept–Apr: Tue–Sun 11am–5pm), an international centre for graphic art and printmaking in Kungsladugården

Left: interior, Gripsholm Castle. **Above:** a castle fit for a Renaissance ruler
Right: decorative detail on a castle cannon

(Royal Barn). There is 2,000 sq m (21,500 sq ft) of space, incorporating exhibition halls and workshops. Check out the print collection and art library, as well as the shop and café. Activities in the centre include seminars, courses and musical events.

Grafikens Hus focuses on the participation of 400 Swedish printmakers, each of whom acquired a 'Konstnärsaktie' (an artist's share or a 'K-share') bought with their own prints. Some 200 K-shares have been offered to artists in the Nordic and Baltic states and Russia. The artists have access to the workshops, which are intended for their work, but are also used as demonstration areas for the public, and for teaching. The café here is a nice place in which to finish the day's sightseeing. It is known for its home-made bread and sweet baked goods, particularly *fruktbullar* (fruit buns) and cinnamon buns.

3 UTÖ *(see map, p54)*

This excursion explores the serene beauty of the outer archipelago. No other island in the archipelago has as rich a history as Utö, which was inhabited even before the Viking era. Although this tour can easily be undertaken in a day, an overnight stay is highly recommended.

To get to Utö in summer, take the boat from Strömkajen. The journey takes about 3 hours. Alternatively, you can take the commuter train line towards Västerhaninge and then feeder bus No 846 to Årstabryggan at Årsta Havsbad. From there, the boat journey takes just 40 minutes. The latter option allows you to travel to Utö in about half the time, but doesn't offer the allure of the leisurely steamboat ride on a perfect summer's day.

Utö has been inhabited since pre-Viking era times and is rich in history. In the 12th century the islanders started to mine iron ore, an activity that went

on until 1879. The miners' story is told in the **Mining Museum** next to Utö Värdhus (Utö Inn). The quaint red wooden cottages on Lurgatan, which are now holiday homes, were the crowded, barely habitable quarters of the miners in the 18th century. It's worth climbing to the windmill, built in 1791, for a fantastic view of the island.

Utö has developed into one of the finest seaside resorts in the Stockholm area and Utö Värdshus has a variety of pleasant accommodation. There is a youth hostel on the island as well as camping and B&B accommodation. You can hire bicycles, rowing boats, canoes and kayaks, and there are regular fishing trips and archipelago safaris.

Utö (Outer Island) enjoys a remote and beautiful location deep in the south-

Left: Utö is both remote and beautiful

ern Stockholm archipelago. It rose out of the sea as a number of small islands at the end of the Ice Age, about 10,000 years ago. The earliest inhabitants were probably nomadic fishers and hunters. The burial grounds at Skogsby on the south island show that there was a permanent settlement here between 550 and 1050. By the end of this period, the whole island was inhabited and iron was being mined. The Utö mines are probably the oldest, and were certainly among the most important, in Sweden, with a heyday lasting more than 700 years. Traces of mining operations can still be seen in the form of some impressive mine shafts. The Nyköping Mine, at 215m (705ft), is the biggest of them all. There are also slag heaps behind the inn.

Artists and Cyclists

When mining was no longer profitable, the island was purchased by the industrial magnate 'Plank Anders'Andersson. He set up a saw mill and timber yard here and made short work of the island's trees. When there was nothing left to exploit, Utö was sold to a merchant by the name of E W Lewin, who did much to make the archipelago attractive to city dwellers. Writers and artists such as Anders Zorn flocked to the island. When Lewin needed accommodation for his summer visitors, the former mining families were forced to vacate their homes on Lurgatan and were housed in a dank building described by one author as 'the prison'. Guided (English) tours supply a more detailed glimpse of Utö's colourful history.

Today, about 200 people live here year-round, but the island's population jumps significantly in the summer when Utö is at its finest. The miles of bicycle paths offer an opportunity to pedal through fragrant meadows and virgin forest, past secluded beaches and towering cliffs. You can explore the smaller islands of **Rånö** and **Nåttarö** by bicycle, for rent near the harbour. If you take the long ride to Ålö, you will be rewarded with a delicious salmon lunch at Båtshaket, right next to the pier where the salmon is caught. Barnensbad beach, about a 1-km (½-mile) walk from the main harbour (where there is another good-value restaurant) is perfect for families.

Adults travelling on their own might prefer the more private cliffs at Rävstavik and Södra Sandvik. The island also offers tennis courts, mini-golf and beach volleyball. You really should not leave the island without sampling Utölimpa, a thick, seeded loaf with a slightly sweet taste, which is unique to Utö. The locals suggest that you cut it in thin slices, and it will last a week or more.

The perfect conclusion to a day of swimming, cycling or sightseeing is dinner at Utö Värdhus, which has a breathtaking view of the sea. You should make a reservation in advance if you want a table with this stunning view. On some summer evenings, there is music and dancing.

Above: don't leave the island without sampling its unique Utölimpa bread

Leisure Activities

SHOPPING

When it comes to shopping, Stockholm has something for everyone. The best shops in the city centre are within easy walking distance and they sell an enormous variety of goods. There is an abundance of small boutiques for fashion and interiors, as well as luxury international designer outlets and well-stocked department stores. It's worth making an effort to visit the market halls, Hörtorgshallen or Östermalmshallen, for Swedish delicacies such as reindeer and elk meat, cloudberries and caviar.

Although you can find good places to shop throughout the city, the most exclusive stores are located in fashionable Östermalm. Gamla Stan is the place to go for handicrafts and unusual knick-knacks. Södermalm has trendy design shops as well as antique and second-hand shops. Vasastan is the place to go for antique bargains.

Opening Hours

Most shops open from 10am to 6pm, Monday to Friday, although many in the city centre stay open until 7pm. The majority are open until 4–5pm on Saturday, the major department stores until 5pm. Large stores, chains, shopping malls, and several notable shops in the city centre are open on Sunday until 3–4pm. Market halls are all closed Sunday and on public holidays.

Tax-Free Shopping

Residents of countries outside the European Union are entitled to a refund of the Value Added Tax they have paid on their purchases. Tax-free shopping on this Global Refund system gives visitors a cash refund of anything between 15 and 18 percent on departure from the European Union. You should look out for the 'Tax-free Shopping' sign. You can get subscribe to the Global Refund scheme at all major departure points, including Arlanda Airport.

Department Stores

Nordiska Kompagniet (NK) is Stockholm's answer to Harrods, a majestic department store in the heart of the city at Hamngatan 18–20. This is as good a place as any to start a shopping tour. NK houses more than 100 outlets under one roof, including fashions, interior decorating, glass and porcelain, kitchenware and underwear.

At the Kungsgatan-Drottningatan corner is PUB, where Greta Garbo once worked, and where Lenin bought his famous cap. Walk south on Drottningatan to Åhléns City, a mid-market department store stocked with virtually everything you could want to buy. Sturegallerian is an exclusive shopping centre at Stureplan in the heart of the city.

Design and Interior Decoration

Designtorget, situated on the ground floor of the Kulturhuset at Sergels Torg (and in Västermalms Galleria on Kungsholmen), is set up as a showcase for budding designers. They apply to be represented, a jury vets them, and the lucky ones' work makes it onto the shelves. There's everything from hats and children's clothes to pottery and sofas. Asplund at Sibyllegatan 31 in Östermalm is home to some of Sweden's best-known designers, such as Pia Wallén, Jonas Bohlin and Tomas Sandell. It's pricy, but it's free to look. Also in Östermalm, Norrgavel at Birger Jarlsgatan 27 showcases Scandinavian furniture design.

Svenskt Tenn, located at the highly fashionable address of Strandvägen 5 in Östermalm, is the city's oldest shop for interior decoration, and has a selection of classic and modern designs. Nordiska Galleriet on Nybrogatan 11, one of the city's oldest furniture shops, has fine furniture from all over the world as well as from local designers such

Left: modern furniture at Nordiska Galleriet
Right: a traditional hand-painted Dalarna horse

as Gunnar Asplund and Mats Theselius. The excellent gift section at the rear can accommodate even an average shopping budget.

Nutida Svenskt Silver (Arsenalsgatan 3) and Galleri Metallum (Hornsgatan 30) in Södermalm are the places for innovative silver creations: jewellery, candlesticks, dishes and much more. At Blås & Knåda at Hornsgatan 26 in Södermalm it's fun to browse through the variety of artistic and everyday objects created by 53 potters and glass blowers. Konsthantverkarna at Mäster Samuelsgatan 2 in Östermalm features attractive silver, glass, pottery and textiles.

Once you find your way to its somewhat funky address at Alströmergatan 20 on Kungsholmen, ROOM is paradise for anyone interested in interior design – and willing to pay for it. Svenskt Glas at Birger Jarlsgatan 8 has a wide selection of items from designers at the leading glass factories. Nordiska Kristall at Kungsgatan 9, in the city, also has a good selection. You can also find Swedish glass, often more competitively priced, in the department stores.

Antiques

Stockholm has preserved a wealth of antiques – in most European countries they would have been lost in war – which are for sale at good prices: try the world's largest auction house – Auktionskompagniet at Regeringsgatan 47. Even if you don't care to bid, browsing among the showrooms sheds light on Swedish homes, the way Swedes live, and what they keep or discard. Antique lovers should check out the shops on Odengatan, Upplandsgatan, and Roslagsgatan.

Fashion

If you are looking for up-market shops and name-dropping labels, you should head for Grev Turegatan, Biblioteksgatan, Birger Jarlsgatan and Norrmalmstorg in Östermalm, Stockholm's answer to Faubourg Saint-Honoré. Here are exclusive international labels – Gucci, Lacoste, Versace, Giorgio Armani and Prada – alongside local talented designers such as Filippa K and Johan Lindeberg. Filippa K, whose store is on Grev Turegatan 18, creates smart, practical clothing for trendy women; Anna Holtblad, at Kungstensgatan 20, makes stylish women's garments. Johan Lindeberg, at Grev Turegatan 9, produces unusual clothing for bold young men. Thalia at Karlavägen 62 is the place to shop for that knock-'em-dead evening dress.

Miss Mary of Sweden, situated at Mäster Samuelsgatan 7, is like a fantasy world of lace, roses and embroidery in white, black, gold and pink. Don't overlook the NK department store for high-quality fashion for both men and women.

Souvenirs and Handicrafts

If you simply must have one of those darling hand-painted red Dalarna horses or any other classic Swedish handicraft, you should take care to shop wisely. For every shop with quality products, there are a dozen with flimsy imitations. Try Svensk Hemslöjd at Sveavägen 44 and Iris Hantverk, both of which are near Hötorget.

The various museum gift shops are also good places for finding souvenirs. The Tourist Centre at Sergels Torg 1 sells an attractive selection of Swedish handicrafts and souvenirs. For Lapp (*Sami*) crafts, visit Carl Wennberg Sameslöjd at Svartmangatan 11 in Gamla Stan. Kilgren Knives and Clothing, also in the Old Town at Västerlånggatan 45, is a good place to look for high-quality handicrafts.

At Österlånggatan 45 is the whimsical Tomtar & Troll, with the handmade elves and trolls that are at the heart of Swedish folklore. Trolls can't stand daylight and come out only at night. Tomtar are small creatures that, if treated with respect, will protect the household from accidents and disaster. The Swedes like to say that every house should have one – just in case.

Left: try a Viking helmet for size

EATING OUT

In the past 10 years or so, Stockholm has become one of Europe's most dynamic and exciting places for eating out. For this we can thank an army of young chefs impeccably trained at the top end of their profession. Of course you can always find **husmanskost** traditional Swedish peasant fare – which these days comes economically but skilfully prepared, with up-market ingredients that give it a new twist.

To experience true husmanskost, sit down to the famous Swedish **smorgasbord**, with salmon, herring, potatoes and dill, meats and crisp bread with hard cheese. And there's always snaps to drink on the side. The best smorgasbord in Stockholm is served at Ulriksdahls Wärdhus, which enjoys a quite wonderful location at Ulriksdahls Slott (Castle; tel: 08-402 61 30), just a short bus ride away from the city centre.

A large number of the chefs at the top-rated restaurants have won international awards in recent years, and seven of the country's restaurants have been awarded Michelin stars. A variety of ethnic styles of cooking are combined to create surprising and delicious dishes generally referred to as 'crossover' cuisine.

More traditional Swedish dishes are often served at lunchtime and they constitute excellent value for money. Look for *dagens rätt* or *dagens lunch* (dish of the day), a meal that usually includes bread, a simple salad,

Above and Right: whatever the time of year, alfresco eating is popular

and soft drink or light beer for a set price of about 70 kr.

For travellers on a tight budget there is no shortage of fast-food outlets, pubs, Chinese restaurants, kebab houses and pizzerias. There are hot-dog kiosks located all over the city; this once-American speciality has become a favourite snack of Stockholmers, particularly when the hot dog is served in a soft wrap-around bread called *tunnbröd*, and complemented with a generous dollop of mashed potatoes.

Key to Prices
The following price key is based on average prices for a three-course meal for one, with half a bottle of house wine, and service and cover charges included. Don't forget to make a prior reservation if you want to eat at one of the more exclusive restaurants.

Very expensive – over 500 kr
Expensive – 400–500 kr
Moderate – 300–400 kr
Inexpensive – under 300 kr

Restaurants

Gondolen

Stadsgården 6, top of Katarina Hissen
Tel: (08) 641 70 90

This is where you will find the city's most fantastic view, and with a menu to match. The cuisine is top-class, particularly the sole flecked with lobster and a buttery dill-lobster sauce, and the toast *skagen*.

Gondolen's adjoining restaurant, Köket, serves superior food in a rustic setting at substantially lower prices. If you don't wish to come here for a meal, you might want to sip a cocktail in the bar and watch the sunset. Very expensive.

Grand's Franska Matsalen

Södra Blasieholmen 8
Tel: (08) 679 35 84

Consistently rated one of the country's best restaurants by the Swedish *Gourmet* magazine, The Grand Hotel's French Dining Room provides an exceptional eating experience – for the incredible view of the Royal Palace as well as the superbly prepared food. There is an emphasis on French cooking, but a Scandinavian menu is also always available. The service is, as you would expect, impeccable. Very expensive.

Operakällaren

Operahuset, Karl XII:s torg
Tel: (08) 676 58 01

With one Michelin star, this is probably Stockholm's best-known restaurant and worth a visit simply for the lavish 19th-century ceiling paintings and Jugendstil bar. Operakällaren (Café Opera) has a state-of-the-art kitchen run by chef Stefano Catenacci. Its afternoon cake buffet is famous. Transforming seasonal ingredients such as pumpkin into delectable and sophisticated dishes, the cooking is anything but predictable. Very expensive.

Pontus In The Green House

Österlånggatan 17
Tel: (08) 545 273 00

Young chef Pontus Frithiof creates culinary masterpieces at his cosy restaurant in Gamla Stan, with an emphasis on fresh fish and shellfish, and indulgences such as caviar and truffles. The home-made bread is probably the best in Sweden and the wine cellar is excellent. The pleasant bistro at street level has lower prices and is the city's best value for a quick lunch, particularly the Asian menu. Very expensive.

Above: Gondolen features the city's best view
Right: Bon Lloc's Mathias Dahlgren

Wedholms Fisk
Nybrokajen 17
Tel: (08) 611 78 74

If you are a connoisseur of seafood, this is the place for you. All the ingredients are carefully selected and prepared according to the classic schools of Swedish and French cuisine. The sauces are excellent, the portions are generous, and the decor sober. Come here for lunch and you'll get good value for your money. Very expensive.

Bon Lloc
Regeringsgatan 111
Tel: (08) 660 60 60

Award-winning chef Mathias Dahlgren has created one of Stockholm's hottest new restaurants with his *nuevo-eurolatino* kitchen (which has roots in Catalonia). The tapas are wonderful, as are creations such as lobster paella and thyme-grilled angler. The oysters, either in the raw or in a creamy soup, are highly recommended. The seven-dish tasting' menu is a good deal, as is the weekday lunch, which you can enjoy for less than 100 kr. Expensive.

Fredsgatan 12
Fredsgatan 12
Tel: (08) 24 80 52

Food as both art and entertainment – such is the hallmark of this award-winning restaurant. Star chef Markus Aujalay creates dishes that are as beautiful to look at as they are to eat. The new menu offers tapas-size dishes only, so be prepared to order several or the seven-course sampler menu. The clientele is fashionable, the decor spare and modern accordingly. Expensive.

Halv Trappa Plus Gård
Lästmakargatan 3
Tel: (08) 678 10 50

The hip 1970s interior design makes this restaurant a magnet for the young and trendy. The cuisine is mainly inspired by China's Sichuan dishes but also features dim sums from Guangzhou and Hong Kong, as well as dishes from various other regions of China. The bar is a nice place to hang out early in the evening, before the crowds arrive. In summer the garden gives a feel of the Riviera. Expensive.

Mårten Trotzig
Västerlånggatan 79
Tel: (08) 442 25 30

You'll find high gastronomic standards at this Gamla Stan restaurant, which consists of several dining rooms – with modern decor – and an attractive courtyard. The clientele is mostly young professionals, who come for either business lunches or relaxed dinners. The chestnut soup is particularly recommended. Expensive.

Sophie's Bar
Biblioteksgatan 5
Tel: (08) 611 84 08

With its safari-theme setting, this venue in the fashionable Östermalm district is the watering hole for the rich and beautiful. It serves top-rate Italian cuisine with a choice of genuine innovations and traditional dishes. The desserts can be sumptuous – try the rum raisin cake served with vanilla ice cream. Expensive.

Bistro Jarl
Birger Jarlsgatan 7
Tel: (08) 611 76 30

A very popular meeting place with the trendy crowd, this is a small, elegant restaurant that specialises in Mediterranean, Swedish and Asian dishes. But Bistro Jarl's biggest claim to fame is that it is the only champagne bar in the whole of Stockholm. Moreover, it offers surprisingly good quality meals for a modest outlay.

In summer, you can sit outdoors and watch the beautiful people as they pass by, perhaps with a glass or two of Taittinger Brut Reserve. Moderate.

Bistro Ruby
Österlånggatan 14
Tel: (08) 20 57 76

If it's a quiet dinner for two that you're after, you can't do better than Bistro Ruby. The restaurant is situated in a romantic medieval cellar in Gamla Stan, and specialises in Texas cuisine. Here you can get perfectly grilled meat with American Southwest trimmings, and fish in different salsas. On Saturdays, you can have an American brunch with eggs Benedict, huevos rancheros and a Bloody Mary. Moderate.

Eriks Bakficka
Fredrikshovsgatan 4
Tel: (08) 660 15 99
Popular with the Östermalm professional crowd, this pleasant, reliable restaurant combines French and Swedish cuisine to create delicious salmon dishes, among others. It is famous for its desserts. A glass of champagne is affordably priced. Moderate.

Storstad
Odengatan 41
Tel: (08) 673 38 00
This restaurant, which serves French and Swedish cuisine, is the place to be seen, with its minimalist decor and crowded bar. The inventive food, comfortable seating and courteous staff make it well worth a visit. Everything, from fish to poultry, is prepared in the most surprising ways. Moderate.

Sturehof
Stureplan 2–4
Tel: (08) 440 57 30
A restaurant and bar situated at the centre of the city's nightlife – and while the food is good, reliable Swedish fare, it is not the main reason why people flock here.

Celebrities, rock stars, fashion designers, and IT geniuses come for the Jonas Bohlin-designed interior, the lively bar and the company around the table. But you won't go wrong ordering Swedish *husmankost* or the fish and shellfish. Moderate.

Bakfickan
Operahuset
Tel: (08) 676 58 09
This little restaurant is a real gem, as its many regular customers, including artists from the Opera House, will attest. The speciality of the house is Swedish home cooking, served over the bar counter, and other meals from the Operakällaren's famous kitchen next door. Inexpensive.

Göken & en Natt
Pontonjärgatan 28
Tel: (08) 654 49 28
You'll receive excellent value for money a this restaurant in Kungsholmen. The cosy atmosphere, friendly service and great view complement the excellent meals, which include everything from traditional Swedish to crossover cuisine. Inexpensive.

Clas På Hörnet
Surbrunnsgatan 20
Tel: (08) 16 51 36
A romantic inn that has been serving superbly prepared classic food since 1731 Today it is exquisitely prepared by chef Nil Emil. Try, for instance, the herring with mashed potatoes or pea soup with sausag and pork. Moderate.

Tranan
Karlsbergsvägen 14
Tel: (08) 527 281 00
A bistro-style restaurant that serves reliabl prepared international cuisine and excellen Swedish home cooking. The bar on the floo below is always lively. Try the *biff Ridberg* or the toast *Pelle Janzon*, and don't overlool the dessert menu. Inexpensive.

Window Bar & Matsal
Norrlandsgatan 33
Tel: (08) 22 47 00
This modern restaurant attracts Sweden' 'Wall Street' crowd during the day an sophisticated city dwellers by night, as result of extremely reasonable prices an well-prepared food. The kitchen feature Asian, Italian, Mexican and Swedis influences, like the *taco* in *wonton* dough filled with fillet of beef and bleak (a sma river fish) roe. Inexpensive.

Left: simple meal, superb setting

NIGHTLIFE

Wild discos, buzzing bars, sedate hotel lounges, rocking clubs, sensational jazz, superb opera and ballet: whatever your taste, Stockholm has it in abundance. The city's nightlife is varied and vibrant, with new venues opening up all the time. Glance at the listings in a daily newspaper and you'll find some 50 to 70 choices among rock clubs alone. This is not surprising, given that Swedish pop music's sometimes significant position on the world stage has made it such an important export item. Stockholm's Globen Arena is a standard stop on the touring schedule of numerous international stars. Most venues are within easy walking distance of each other and the centre so, whether you're enjoying *La Traviata* at the Opera House or some modern jazz at an intimate club in Gamla Stan, you should not have far to go.

Stockholm has a lively theatrical life. The legendary film and theatre director Ingmar Bergman still produces plays at the Royal Dramatic Theatre. However, nearly all of the city's dramatic performances are in Swedish, which makes theatre in Stockholm inaccessible to most tourists. Ask at SIS (the Stockholm Information Service, tel: 789 2490) about shows that might be staged in English, particularly during the summer.

Nightclubs and discos usually start to get lively at 10 or 11pm and generally close between 3 and 5am. Unfortunately, many nightclubs have long queues outside from 9pm or 10pm, even if they are not full inside. This is an irritating way of showing that the club is popular. Avoid the queues by arriving early, or book a table for dinner so that you don't have to pay the entrance fee.

Booking Tickets

Tickets for an event can usually be bought at the theatre or sporting arena. You can also book in advance with the help of your hotel, a Stockholm Information Service tourist office, or at a ticket agency, such as Biljett Direkt (tel: 077-170 70 70). Be warned that you might have to pay a nominal booking fee at an agency.

Classical Music

Berwaldhallen
Dag Hammarskjölds väg 3
Tel: (08) 784 50 00
World-class classical music is played here regularly by the Swedish Radio Symphony Orchestra, the Swedish Radio Chorus and guest orchestras.

Konserthuset
Hörtorget 8
Tel: (08) 786 02 00
Home of the Royal Philharmonic Orchestra, an internationally acclaimed 100-piece orchestra currently led by American conductor Alan Gilbert.

Above: Gamla Stan is a focal point for the city's excellent, intimate jazz clubs

Jazz and Blues

Fasching Jazzclubb
Kungsgatan 63
Tel: (08) 534 829 60
The city's foremost club for jazz, blues, funk and Latin music, with performances nearly every day of the week.

Glenn Miller Café
Brunnsgatan 21A
Tel: (08) 10 03 22
Intimate jazz café with a New York atmosphere; live music Mon–Sat.

Lydmar Hotel
Sturegatan 10
Tel: (08) 566 113 00
The Lydmar hotel bar has one of the city's best stages for top artists. Attracts a young, trendy crowd.

Nalen
Regeringsgatan 74
Tel: (08) 505 292 00
An illustrious 1950s venue that only recently re-opened; featuring not only live jazz, but swing, blues and big band.

Stampen
Stora Nygatan 5
Tel: (08) 20 57 94
A classic jazz spot that attracts a somewhat older clientele.

Opera

Confidencen
Ulriksdals Slottsteater
Tel: (08) 85 70 16
Sweden's oldest rococo theatre stages weekly opera and ballet at Ulriksdal Slott (Castle) June–Sept.

Drottningholm Slottsteater
Drottningholm Palace
Tel: (08) 556 931 00
In the summer, major operas are presented at this 18th-century theatre, which still uses the original stage settings and machinery.

Kungliga Operan
Gustav Adolfs Torg
Tel: (08) 24 82 40
Traditional productions in the original language with some lunchtime operas or concerts in the Gustav III opera café.

Dance

Dansens Hus
Barnhusgatan 12–14
Tel: (08) 508 990 90
The largest dance stage in northern Europe. Many established companies make guest appearances here.

Kungliga Operan
Gustav Adolfs Torg
Tel: (08) 24 82 40
Top-class classical ballet at this 100-year-old theatre, with favourites such as *Swan Lake*, *The Nutcracker* and *Romeo and Juliet*.

Moderna Dansteatern
Slupskjulsvägen, 32 Torpedverkstan
Skeppsholmen
Tel: (08) 611 32 33
An important stage for modern dance, in an old torpedo factory on Skeppsholmen.

Film

Virtually all foreign films are screened in their original language, with Swedish subtitles – inferior dubbing is not a popular option. Local newspapers have full details of films and times. Book a ticket in advance through the websites of the two major film companies: SF (www.sf.se) and Sandrews (www.sandrewmetronome.se).

Above: Sturecompagniet stays open until 5am

Bars

Cadier Bar
Grand Hotel
Södra Blasieholmshamnen 8
Tel: (08) 679 35 00
The most elegant bar in Stockholm, the Cadier is appropriately located in a plush five-star hotel. Listen to the gentle tinkling of the grand piano while admiring the view from the veranda of the Royal Palace and archipelago.

Lydmar Hotel
Sturegatan 10
Tel: (08) 566 113 00
This is the watering hole for the city's trendy artists, designers and musicians – who always seem to know which drinks are the latest fashion.

Operabaren
Kungsträdgården
Tel: (08) 676 58 00
Feast your eyes on the Jugendstil decor while sitting back on the leather sofa and sipping an expertly mixed martini. This classy joint sometimes becomes crowded, so you should arrive early if you want a place by the bar. Closed mid-July to early August.

Sheraton Lobby Lounge
Tegelbacken 6
Tel: (08) 412 34 00
A classic international bar that is perfect for business travellers who want to relax with piano music and a cocktail.

Sturehof's Obar
Stureplan 2
Tel: (08) 440 57 30
The crowded outer bar is frequented by local celebrities. The inner bar features unusual decor and a more mature clientele. The outdoor area in summer is the hottest place to be and be seen.

Clubs

Café Opera
Operahuset
Kungsträdgården
Tel: (08) 676 58 07
Stockholm's best-known club, although its heyday was in the 1980s. Now, however, after some years of lying low, it is once again attracting a mixed clientele of young and old, trendy and staid.

Chiaro
Birger Jarlsgatan 24
Tel: (08) 678 00 09
An eclectic selection of modern music is performed on several dance floors for a young crowd.

Spy Bar
Birger Jarlsgatan 20
Tel: (08) 545 037 01
A hot nightclub known for attracting local and international celebrities, including the Swedish crown princess. But it is a victim of its own success – the average person has to wait in often long queues while the VIPs breeze through the door.

Sturecompagniet
Sturegatan 4
Tel: (08) 545 034 48
A large disco on several floors, and a rock club on street level. A favourite of local soap stars and the young and trendy. Open until 5am; expect long queues.

Tiger
Kungsgatan 18
Tel: (08) 24 47 00
A popular club with elegant restaurant, three bars and live music. Thur–Sat from 7pm.

Above: there is no shortage of nightclubs for revellers of all persuasions

CALENDAR OF EVENTS

Stockholm's beauty can be appreciated throughout the year, whether in the long days of summer or against the winter backdrop of shimmering snow and ice. The country's national festivals are celebrated in traditional ways in Stockholm and are highly popular with locals and tourists alike. This is a city of festivals, where celebrations concentrate on everything from food to art and music. The city's numerous international fairs – featuring antiques, boating, camping and other such leisure pursuits – are also usually well worth visiting.

When it comes to sport, Stockholm is home to many world-class events. No matter what time of year you visit the city, you will find an abundance of activities to keep you entertained.

Specific dates for many of the following events vary from year to year. The Stockholm Tourist Centre & Excursion Shop (tel: 789 24 90, www.stockholmtown.com) will be able to give you exact dates.

January
The Antiques Fair, the year's first major event, is held at Stockholm International Fairs, Älvsjö

February
The Sweden Hockey Games is an ice hockey tournament at Globen. Competing teams come from Russia, the Czech Republic and Finland, and also include the Swedish national team, Tre Kronor.

International athletes gather at the Globen arena for the **GE Gala**, one of the world's top indoor competitions.

The Stockholm Art Fair has works of art (for sale) at Sollentuna Exhibition Centre.

March
Stockholm International Boat Show is the spring's major boat exhibition at Stockholm International Fairs in Älvsjö.

Liljevalchs Konsthall on Djurgården holds its annual art exhibition, **the Spring Salon**, featuring new artists.

April
Walpurgis Night at Skansen on *30 April* involves traditional celebrations with folk dancing, torchlight processions, student choirs, bonfires and fireworks.

The King's Birthday is also celebrated on *30 April* with a military parade from the Royal Palace.

May
Round Lidingö Race is a long-distance sailing event with hundreds of boats of all shapes and sizes.

Tjejtrampet is a 40-km (25-mile) cycling event at Gärdet, with 7,000 female cyclists.

Historical Festival features a diverse range of activities and is held in Gamla Stan, and on Riddarholmen and Helgeandsholmen.

Above: youngsters celebrate National Day (6 June)

June

Stockholm Marathon is one of the 10 biggest marathons in the world, with about 13,000 runners.

At the annual **Restaurant Festival** Kungsträdgården becomes the world's largest outdoor restaurant.

National Day on 6 June is traditionally celebrated at Skansen in the presence of the royal family.

Midsummer's Eve is a major Swedish festival celebrated over three days at Skansen. It begins at 2pm on Midsummer's Eve with the traditional raising of the maypole and ring dancing.

Drottningholms Slottsteater opens its summer season of concerts, operas and dance in the 18th-century court theatre.

Music at the Palace heralds the start of the summer concert season in the Hall of State and the Royal Chapel at Kungliga Slottet (Royal Palace).

July

Round Gotland Race is a major international sailing event with a start and finish at Sandhamn.

Stockholm Jazz Festival is widely known for featuring some of the biggest names in jazz, who play in a stunning outdoor setting on Skeppsholmen.

August

Crayfish Season opens the last week of August as Swedes eat crayfish and sing snaps songs'.

Stockholm Pride Festival, a gay and lesbian celebration, is held at Tantolunden.

September

The Stockholm Cup is a horse race at the Täby course with an international field.

October

Lidingö Race is the world's largest cross-country event, with tens of thousands of competitors, including elite runners, senior citizens and children.

November

Stockholm Open is an ATP tennis tournament held at Kungliga Tennishallen.

The Stockholm Film Festival brightens the darkening days of winter with a 10-day event of public screenings and the presentation of awards.

Stockholm International Horse Show at Globen is a dressage and jumping World Cup competition that is entertaining even for those not usually interested in horses.

December

On **Nobel Day**, 10 December, the year's Nobel Prize laureates are honoured in a ceremony at Konserthuset (Concert Hall). In the evening, the royal family attends a banquet at Stadshuset (City Hall).

The country's **Lucia Celebrations**, which take place on 13 December, honour the white-clad Lucia, known as the 'Queen of Light', together with her girl attendants and 'star boys'. Lucia herself serves the Nobel laureates early-morning coffee with saffron buns, and she also sings traditional songs. In the evening a Lucia procession wends its way through the city to the celebrations and fireworks at Skansen. Many Swedish homes, schools and workplaces have their own Lucia celebrations.

Christmas markets are traditionally large affairs at Skansen, Rosendals Slott, Stortorget (in Gamla Stan) and Drottningholms Slott.

Christmas is by far the most treasured of all the traditional Swedish holidays. The main celebration takes place on Christmas Eve and features an abundant smorgasbord, followed by the presentation of gifts, which are usually delivered by a family member disguised as Father Christmas.

Right: Midsummer's Eve is the most traditional of festivals

Practical
Information

GEOGRAPHY

Sweden is the fourth largest country in Europe, covering 486,661 sq km (187, 900 sq miles). It is a long, thin country, about the size of the state of California. The southernmost point is on the same latitude as Edinburgh and the northernmost point is 280km (175 miles) north of the Arctic Circle. This accounts for the glaciers in the far north. More than 60 percent of the country is forest. The most recent Ice Age is responsible for creating its archipelago and smoothing the rocks along the coastline.

Sweden borders Norway to the west and Finland in the east. Since 2000 it has been connected to Denmark – Scandinavia's other country – in the south by the Öresund Bridge. The capital city, Stockholm, is in the southeast. The city is built on islands which separate the Baltic Sea from Lake Mälaren.

POPULATION

Stockholm is the largest city in Sweden, with a population of more than 760,000. The Greater Stockholm region has more than 1.8 million inhabitants. This area is the powerhouse of Sweden, accounting for more than one-fifth of the country's employment and a quarter of its total production. In many countries, this would make Stockholm a noisy industrial city but Sweden's expansive countryside means there is space enough for everyone, and more.

WEATHER

Stockholm's maritime climate is quite varied and every season has its particular pleasures. One distinguishing feature is the short, dark winter days and the long, light summer days. Winters can be relatively mild, or heavy snowfall may lie on the ground until March. In winter the temperature falls below freezing but it is rarely severely cold. At the beginning

Left: the T-banan subway
Right: another popular way to travel

of April, spring makes its long-awaited debut and a month later the birch trees and the city's outdoor cafés have blossomed.

Summer arrives sometime in June, certainly by Midsummer's Eve (late in the month). The weather in summer is unpredictable. It is usually cool and sometimes it rains, but in a good year visitors can enjoy remarkably high temperatures for northern Europe. During July and August the water in Stockholm stays at a relatively mild temperature, and is perfect for bathing.

In September, summer turns to autumn as the leaves change from green to red and the air becomes bracing and cool.

Temperatures
Winter: -7–2°C (19–36°F)
Spring: 5–5°C (41–59°F)
Summer: 15–25°C (59–77°F)
Autumn: 0–8°C (32–64°F)

GETTING THERE

By Air
Your best chance for getting a good deal on a ticket is to be flexible about departure and arrival dates and to book well in advance; low-season fares are substantially cheaper. Most major European cities and several North American ones have direct flights to Stockholm.

Many of the world's leading airlines and Swedish domestic flights serve Arlanda Airport, located about 40km (25 miles) north of the city centre.

Stockholm is served by two other airports. Bromma, close to the city centre, is used by a few of the smaller domestic airlines, such as Malmö Aviation, with flights from London via Malmö. Skavsta, about 100km (62 miles) south of Stockholm near Nykoping, is used by Ryanair and others for budget-price flights to and from London Stansted Airport. A bus takes travellers into Stockholm.

Services between Stockholm and North America are operated by SAS (Scandinavian Airlines), Finnair, Icelandair, by the US airline Continental (starting June 2005) and other airlines such as KLM and Malaysian Airlines.

From the Airport
Taxis

Taxis are available from the ground floor of Arlanda Airport. Most taxi firms have a fixed charge of about 350 kr for the 25-minute trip to the city centre. You should avoid the so-called 'black' or illegal taxis and check the fare before departure.

Bus

The Flygbussarna shuttle bus service operates every 10 minutes at peak times. The journey to the City Terminal at Central Station takes about 45 minutes and costs about 90 kr.

Rail

The shortest journey is by the Arlanda Express train, which costs 180 kr for the 20-minute trip to Central Station. There are two stations at the airport, one for terminals 2, 3, 4 and the other for terminal 5. Arlanda's Sky City station is served by long-distance trains.

Car hire

While most of the itineraries recommended in this book are best taken either on foot or by public transport, you might want to hire a car for excursions outside the city. A number of car hire companies operate at the airport, including the following:

Avis tel: (08) 797 99 70
Europcar tel: (08) 593 609 40
Hertz tel: (08) 797 99 00

By Rail and Coach

Rail travel from much of Europe to Stockholm is quite quick, comfortable and inexpensive. The journey time has been reduced considerably since the opening of the Öresund Bridge between Denmark and Sweden which carries both rail and road traffic. Travel agencies can provide more details on available options.

Within Sweden, the state-owned railway company Statens Järnvägar operates many of the long-distance trains. Some routes are operated by private companies such as Tågkompaniet (Stockholm-northern Sweden). The X2000 high-speed train is a competitive alternative to air travel. The journey from Malmö to Stockholm takes about five hours and from Gothenburg three hours.

For further information in Sweden, call Statens Järnvägar (SJ), tel: (0771) 75 75 75, or Tågkompaniet, tel: (020) 444 111. In the UK call Eurostar, tel: (08705) 186 186.

The same routes are served by express coaches such as Swebus. The journey is longer – about 7 hours from Gothenburg and 9 hours from Malmö – but the fares are much cheaper and advance booking is not necessary.

By Road

Visitors arriving in Sweden from Denmark can use the impressive new Öresund toll bridge

between Copenhagen and Malmö. On the Swedish side the bridge connects with the E4, a 550-km (340-mile) motorway to Stockholm. Alternatively, take a 20-minute ferry ride from Helsingor (Denmark) to Helsingborg (Sweden).

Car ferries to Gothenburg operate from Frederikshavn (Denmark) and Kiel (Germany) with an onward, 450-km (280-mile) journey on the E3 to Stockholm. The quickest option from Germany to Sweden is the catamaran ferry from Rostock to Trelleborg in southern Sweden, then the E6 to Malmö and E4 to Stockholm.

Speed limits on Swedish motorways are 110kmh (68mph); 90 kmh (56 mph) on other major roads. In densely populated areas the speed limit is 50–70kmh (30–42mph). Watch out when you're driving in the countryside, especially at dawn and dusk, because elk and deer can suddenly appear on the road.

TRAVEL ESSENTIALS

Visas and Passports
A valid passport entitles you to stay for up to three months, and visas are not normally required. From 2001, passports will not be needed by visitors from European countries that signed the Schengen agreement.

Customs
Swedish customs formalities are usually quite painless and baggage is rarely opened, but it's sensible to observe the duty free limits and other rules. Visitors from European Union countries can bring in (tax paid) 10 litres of spirits or 20 litres of fortified wine, 90 litres of wine plus 110 litres of beer. Visitors from non-EU countries can take in 1 litre of spirits or 2 litres of fortified wine, plus 2 litres of wine. The allowance for cigarettes is 800 for EU residents and 200 for those from non-EU countries. All visitors can take in 15 litres of strong beer.

All visitors can bring in canned foods; EU citizens can also bring up to a maximum of 5kg (11lb) of fresh food per person; visitors from other areas must have a certificate from a recognised exporter. Visitors from non-EU countries can also bring goods up to a value of 1,700 kr, in addition to normal travel-related items. Tax-free sales in Sweden are permitted only for travellers with a final destination beyond the borders of the EU.

GETTING AROUND

If you intend to travel on public transport during your stay, the Stockholmskort (Stockholm card) is a good deal. This passport to the city can be purchased for a period of one, two or three days and gives free admission to a host of museums and attractions, plus of course free travel on local buses, trains and the underground. It also allows free city-centre parking in metered spaces and bonus offers and discounts. The card can be purchased at tourist information offices at Sergels Torg and Central Station, other tourist information offices in the Stockholm region, and at various camping grounds, hostels, and SL centres.

Buses
The local bus network in Stockholm is claimed to be the world's largest. It is operated by the Stockholm Transit Authority, which also runs the underground and local mainline train services. Instead of paying cash on the bus, it is cheaper to buy a *förköpshäfte*, which is a voucher for 10 journeys within the city centre. The driver will stamp your ticket when you start and you are allowed to travel, without incurring any further costs, within one zone on the bus, train and underground for an hour on the same ticket.

Alternatively, you could purchase the SL Tourist Card, which offers free travel on public transport in the Greater Stockholm area for a period of 24 or 72 hours. The 72-hour card includes free admission to Gröna Lund Tivoli and Kaknäs Tower.

Buses provide a pleasant and economical way to see the city. The best sightseeing routes are 3, 4, 46, 47, 62 and 69, which cover most of the central area and many sights. Routes 47 and 69 from Norrmalmstorg, are useful for sights not served by the underground. Route 47 takes visitors to Djurgården, with the attractions of Skansen, Gröna Lund, Vasamuseet, and Nordiska Museet, continuing to Waldemarsudde. Route 69 travels to southern Gärdet with its many sights, including Kaknäs Tower, the city's highest point, and Thielska Galleriet.

Underground
Stockholm is justifiably proud of its underground railway, known as T-banan (the T stands for tunnel – all stations are identified

Left: Central Station

by the T sign). The T-banan is spotless, and more than 100 stations cover more than 95km (60 miles). Stockholm's underground is unique in one way: it is the world's longest art gallery. Half of the stations have paintings, sculptures, mosaics or engravings created by more than 70 artists.

Trams

In the summer months, lovingly restored vintage trams operate on the former Route 7 between Norrmalmstorg and Djurgården, where 14 trams are stabled. Every year more than 300,000 passengers enjoy this old-fashioned method of travel. Refreshments are served on some services.

USEFUL INFORMATION

Tourist Information

The main office of Stockholm Tourist Centre & Excursion Shop is located at Segels Torg 1 (June–Aug: Mon–Fri 9am–7pm, Sat 9am–5pm, Sun 10am–4pm; Oct–Apr: Mon–Fri 9am–6pm, Sat–Sun 10am–3pm; May and Sept: Mon–Fri 9am–6pm, Sat, Sun 10am–4pm). If in doubt while on the road, you should look out for the green 'i' sign which indicates authorised tourist information offices at other city locations.

A publication *What's on in Stockholm* is distributed every month free of charge and is available from tourist offices and most hotels. Before you leave home it's a good idea to obtain the latest information about Stockholm from the internet. For example you could consult SIS's excellent website, www.stockholmtown.com

Disabled visitors

Stockholm is a wheelchair-friendly city with frequent ramp access to public transport and buildings. The stop lights 'chirp' to assist the sight-impaired at road crossings.

Children

The public transport system and other amenities were created with families in mind. Stockholm is great for children. Navigating a pushchair in Stockholm is no problem as there are ramps leading down to subway stations and city buses automatically lower a platform in the rear to admit pushchairs and prams. Many toilets in the city have changing facilities, while post offices and banks often have a corner with books and toys for children. The city parks usually loan out bicycles and sand-pit toys for free.

Many of the itineraries recommended in this book can be enjoyed by families, but if you're looking for excursions for the youngest children in particular, the following should appeal.

The top choice is Junibacken (Tue–Fri 10am–5pm, Sat–Sun 9am–6pm; extended hours in July; tel: 587 230 00), the children's museum at Gälarparken on Djurgården, which is dedicated to the work of Astrid Lindgren. Whether or not your children are acquainted with Pippi Longstocking, they will enjoy the tram ride, with an English recording, that takes visitors through Astrid's World, with models of scenes from her books, incorporating lights, sounds and moving figures, sometimes deliciously scary. The tram ride finishes with a visit to Pippi's home, where children can dress up and play inside or climb on a huge horse. Ongoing exhibits offer more opportunity for hands-on play. There is a well-stocked children's bookshop and a restaurant.

Another popular choice is Gröna Lund (30 Apr–mid Sept, hours vary) the Victorian amusement park on Djurgården with all the usual thrills of a mid-sized European amusement park, in a pretty waterfront setting.

At the Nordiska Museet, the Children's Playhouse (Mon–Fri 10am–4pm, Sat–Sun 11am–5pm) gives youngsters the opportunity to dress up in period clothing, ride a horse and carriage, shop at the general store, prepare food in a kitchen, draw water from a well, or milk a cow. The playhouse is often crowded at weekends and during winter, when it's a favourite outing for Stockholm families.

The Kulturhuset (Culture House, Tues–Fri 10am–6pm, Sat–Sun 11am–5pm) features a

Above: the tram travels from Norrmalmstorg to Djurgården

Children's Room that offers the opportunity to paint or make crafts for a nominal fee, with friendly staff on hand to help out.

Balloon Rides

Stockholm is one of the few world capitals in which you can fly in a hot-air balloon over the city centre. On a clear summer night, the sky is full of colourful balloons. Traditionally, balloon outings end with a presentation of diplomas, a picnic and champagne. If you care to try this form of aerial sightseeing, contact one of the following companies:

Air Ballooning tel: (08) 704 84 94
Ballongflyg tel: (08) 92 02 02
City Ballong tel: (08) 34 54 64 (make reservations at the Utflyksbutiken in the Tourist Centre & Excursion Shop)
Far & Flyg tel: (08) 645 7700
Upp & Ner tel: (08) 462 03 80

MONEY MATTERS

Currency

Sweden's currency is the krona (plural kronor), abbreviated to SEK or kr, and divided into 100 öre. The smallest coin is 50 öre; the largest note is 1,000 kronor. It's best not to carry notes of more than 500 kronor.

As Sweden remains outside the European Monetary Union (EMU), the Euro is not used (with exceptions).

Changing Money

Stockholm has various bureaux de change chains that generally provide a better rate than the banks. Changing money at a hotel is expensive. Always check rates and commission charges, which can vary significantly. Currency can be changed at the X-change outlets at Arlanda Airport 5.30am–11.30pm, and at the Central Station 7am–9pm; more outlets can be found in PUB department store and on Kungsgatan.

FOREX, with its bright yellow sign, does not charge a commission. FOREX booths are located at Arlanda Airport, Central Station and elsewhere.

Travellers' cheques are widely accepted, as are leading credit cards, by most hotels, shops and restaurants. The city has lots of ATM machines for cash withdrawals.

Hours and Holidays

Business hours are Mon–Fri 9am–5pm; city shopping hours are generally Mon–Fri 10am–7pm, Sat 10am–4pm, Sun noon–3pm.

Most museums and other attractions are open either from 10am to 5pm or from 11am to 6pm throughout the year, although there are longer opening hours during the summer season. The majority are usually closed on Mondays. See individual entries for more specific times.

Public Holidays

1 January	New Year's Day
6 January	Epiphany
late March/April	Good Friday and Easter Monday
1 May	Labour Day
late May	Ascension Day
early June	Pentecost (10 days after Ascension)
Weekend closest to 24 June	
	Midsummer
1 November	All Saints' Day
24/5 December	Christmas

If the holiday falls either two days before or after the weekend, offices and businesses tend to be closed on the intermediate day (which is known as a *klämdag* or 'squeeze day').

The whole month of July has become an unofficial holiday, because this is the time when most office employees are on summer leave. This is not the time of year to conduct important business in Stockholm.

Right: an entertainer in Gröne Lund

HEALTH & EMERGENCIES

The emergency telephone number for police, fire and ambulance is 112. It can be dialled free of charge from all public telephones, but should only be used in case of emergency.

For minor illnesses or other concerns, you can call the Healthcare Information Service (Sjukvårdsupplysningen), tel: 463 91 00, which is open 24 hours a day.

No particular vaccinations are needed by anyone planning a visit to Sweden. Several city hospitals have accident and emergency clinics. These include Karolinska Sjukhuset, Astrid Lindgrens Barnsjukhus (for children), Danderyds Sjukhus, St Eriks Sjukhus (for optical and dental emergencies), St Göran's Sjukhus (which is privately owned) and Södersjukhuset.

Contact the Health Information Service – which provides a service in English and can assign patients to the appropriate hospital or duty doctor – before visiting an emergency clinic. If you don't make use of this free service, you can experience long queues. Citizens of eu countries are entitled to free medical care if they produce an E111 form and a valid passport or other form of identification. Not all treatment is covered by the E111, however, so it is worth taking out private medical insurance before travelling.

The state-run pharmacies (apotek) can dispense medicines for most minor ailments without a prescription, and the staff can usually give good advice on appropriate medication. Pharmacies are normally open Mon–Fri 8.30am–4pm or 6pm. Some also open on Sat. The cw Scheele pharmacy near the Central Station is open 24 hours a day, seven days a week.

POST & TELECOMMUNICATIONS

Telephone

The Stockholm area code is 08. Public telephone kiosks, owned by the state-run Telia company, are usually operated by card only. You can purchase the cards at newspaper kiosks and in shops throughout the city. They are available in 30, 60 and 100 units. For a local call, one unit buys one minute, whereas other calls cost two units per minute.

Alternatively, you can use normal credit cards or international telephone cards. You can make reverse-charge calls from all public phones. You will find English-language directions on how to use the phone, but unfortunately there are no directories. To obtain a number you don't know, you should dial Eniro directory enquiries on tel: 118 118.

Calling Overseas

To place an international call from Sweden, dial 00 + country code + area code (omitting any initial 0) + local number.

Mobile Phones

Telephone kiosks in Stockholm are a victim of modern techonology – they are rapidly declining in number because virtually everybody in the city now has a mobile phone. In most cases, foreign visitors can use gsm phones in Sweden. Within the Stockholm area you should dial the area code 08 before the local number; the country code is not needed.

Postal Services

Post offices have been phased out gradually and their services taken over by grocery stores, convenience stores and petrol stations. The majority are open seven days a week from 9am to 9pm. A small number of Post Centres are open 5 to 6 days a week between 7am and 7pm. You can purchase stamps at Pressbyrån kiosks and from most tourist information offices.

It costs 5.5 kr to send a postcard or a letter that weighs less than 20g (0.04lb) within Sweden; 10 kr to other European countries and the rest of the world. Post boxes are painted different colours: yellow boxes are for mail to destinations abroad and the rest of Sweden; blue boxes for letters within the Stockholm area (post codes beginning with 1).

Left: even the police travel on bicycles

Useful Addresses

Tourist Centre & Excursion Shop
Segels Torg 1
Tel: (08) 508 28 508; from abroad: (46 8) 508 28 508
Fax: (08) 508 28 509
Info@svb.stockholm.se
www.stockholmtown.com

Hotellcentralen (Hotel Bookings)
Central Station
Oct–Apr: Mon–Sat 9am–6pm, Sun noon–4pm;
June–Aug: daily 8am–8pm;
Sept and May: daily 9am–6pm.
Tel: (08) 508 28 508
Fax: (08) 791 86 66

**De Handikappades Riksförbund
(Information for disabled visitors)**
Tel: (08) 685 80 00
Info@dhr.se

City Sightseeing (Guided tours by bus)
Gustav Adolfs Torg
Tel: (08) 587 140 20

Stockholm Sightseeing (Guided tours by boat)
Strömkajen, Grand Hotel
Tel: (08) 587 140 20

Taxiguiding (Licensed taxi guides)
Tel: (020) 20 20 20; (08) 15 00 00

ACCOMMODATION

Whether you're travelling for pleasure or on business, in a large group or as an independent visitor, it is a good idea to make an early reservation through Hotellcentralen (The Hotel Centre). Hotellcentralen is Stockholm's official tourist accommodation agency and is one of Stockholm Visitors Board's authorised tourist offices. The agency works with all hotels regardless of price category or chain affiliation and has specialised knowledge of communications, tariffs, types of room and other hotel facilities. Booking is free of charge and can be done by telephone, fax, e-mail or via the internet.

Many hotels have attractive summer and weekend rates and some also offer 'last-minute reductions' – enquire when you make your reservation. It's also worth looking into the Stockholm Package, a value-for-money deal covering 55 hotels in a range of prices. It includes accommodation (two extra beds for children under 18 at no extra charge) and breakfast, plus the Stockholm Card, which includes the entrance fee to 70 attractions around the city as well as unlimited free travel on local subways, buses, local trains and tour boats. The Stockholm Package can be booked on all days of the week from 1 June to 31 Aug and at weekends and holidays during the rest of the year.

Hotellcentralen is located at the Central Station and is open daily. For further information, tel: (46 8) 508 28 508, fax: (46 8) 791 86 66, e-mail: hotels@svb.stockholm.se or visit the website at www.stockholmtown.com/hotels

Stockholm has an excellent selection of accommodation in various price ranges. Many of the leading hotels have first-class business facilities. The following is a list of selected accommodation that is divided into four price categories:

$$$$ = $350 and over
$$$ – $200–$350
$$= $100–$200
$ = under $100

Prices are for a standard double room, although in the budget category ($), many are for a bed in a shared dormitory or basic single room. All are located within the city limits of Stockholm. If you are calling a hotel while you are in Stockholm, remember that you do not need to use the 08 prefix.

Berns Hotel
Näckströmsgatan 8
Tel: (08) 556 322 50
Fax: (08) 566 322 01
hotelberns@berns.se
This trendy and centrally located hotel was recently revamped by British interior-design architect Sir Terence Conran. It is a small, friendly and exclusive hotel that prides itself on the quality of its personal service. There are 65 rooms, and three suites (one with sauna). Many rooms have a balcony with a wonderful city view. Guests have free access and a separate entrance to the fitness centre at the Grand Hotel. The adjacent restaurant and bar is well worth a visit, particularly for its shellfish. $$$$

Diplomat Hotel
Strandvägen 7C
Tel: (08) 459 68 00
Fax: (08) 459 68 20
Info@diplomathotel.com
www.diplomathotel.com
This small, first-class, family-owned hotel is on one of the most elegant avenues, facing the waterfront. Built in 1911 in classic Jugendstil it has 128 rooms and suites of four-star quality, with particularly elegant bathrooms. The teahouse for which the hotel is famous has now been modernised as the T/Bar, and also serves breakfast, lunch and dinner. $$$$

Grand Hotel Stockholm
S Blasieholmshamnen 8
Tel: (08) 679 3500
Fax: (08) 611 86 86
hotel.grand@grandhotel.se
www.grandhotel.se
This 5-star hotel has an unparalleled view of Lake Mälaren and the Royal Palace, and attracts visiting celebrities and executives. There are 310 individually furnished rooms, including 21 suites, and a Business Centre. Many rooms have ISDN sockets. There's a modern gym with dry and steam saunas and massages. The Franska Matsalen (French Dining Room) is one of Stockholm's top restaurants. The sumptuous breakfast buffet is justifiably famous. $$$$

Nordic Light Hotel & Nordic Sea Hotel
Vasaplan
Tel: (08) 505 630 00
Fax: (08) 505 630 60

info@nordichotels.se
www.nordichotels.se
These two first-class hotels of ultra-modern Scandinavian design were opened in 2001. The 175-room Nordic Light features 19 'light beds' equipped with advanced color lighting. 'Love Packages' offer couples a romantic stay with chocolate-covered fruit, champagne and breakfast in bed. For this, the hotel won *Elle UK*'s prestigious title 'World's Sexiest Hotel' in 2004.

The Nordic Sea Hotel, with a huge fish tank in the lobby, features comfort and simplicity in all of its 367 rooms. There are two bars, the C-Bar and the Icebar – the world's first permanent ice bar, kept at -5° all year round. Interior fittings, including the glasses, are made of pure ice from the Torne River in northern Sweden. Both hotels are centrally located beside the Arlanda Express terminal. $$$$

Victory Hotel
Lilla Nygatan 5
Tel: (08) 506 400 00
Fax: (08) 506 400 10
Info@victory-hotel.se
www.victory-hotel.se
The flagship of the Tre Hotell i Gamla Stan chain, the 5-star Victory has an Admiral Nelson theme: a letter to Lady Hamilton is one of many rare treasures. There are 48 rooms, including four suites, each elegantly appointed and with its own interesting history. The Leijontornet Restaurant is highly recommended. $$$$

First Hotel Reisen
Skeppsbron 12
Tel: (08) 22 32 60
Fax: (08) 20 15 59
reisen@firsthotels.se
www.firsthotels.com
This old Gamla Stan building is in a lovely location on Skeppsbron. It has 144 rooms and a popular piano bar, and the Primo Ciao Ciao Restaurant serves the city's best pizzas. $$$

Lady Hamilton Hotel
Storkyrkobrinken 5
Tel: (08) 506 401 00
Fax: (08) 506 401 10
Info@lady-hamilton.se
www.lady-hamilton.se
This Class A-listed building in Gamla Stan was built in 1407 and converted from a private home

Left: the Grand Hotel flies the flag

in 1975. Take a dip in the 14th-century basement well. The 34 rooms are individually decorated with folk art and maritime antiques. Double rooms have cable TV, film channels, mini-bar, internet and computer facilities. $$$

Lydmar Hotel
Sturegatan 10
Tel: (08) 556 113 00
Fax: (08) 566 113 01
Info@lydmar.se/www.lydmar.se
This 62-room hotel near the city centre and the trendy Stureplan neighbourhood emphasises quality in rooms decorated with antiques and modern art. It hosts regular jazz evenings and stages art exhibitions. The restaurant serves delicious food with the accent on Mediterranean and Californian cooking. $$$

Scandic Sergel Plaza Hotel
Brunkebergstorg 9
Tel: (08) 517 263 00
Fax: (08) 517 263 11
sergel.plaza@scandic-hotels.com
www.scandic-hotels.se
'Hotel of the Year' four times since it was remodelled in 1984, this large hotel offers a full range of services for tourists and business travellers. There are 405 rooms and 12 suites. On the Executive Floor, you have a choice of Japanese breakfast or buffet, plus a robe and morning paper. The Anna Bella Restaurant is rated among the very best in Sweden. $$$

Radisson SAS Royal Viking Hotel
Vasagatan 1
Tel: (08) 506 540 00
Fax: (08) 506 540 01
sales.royal.stockholm@radissonsas.com
www.radissonsas.com
In the heart of Stockholm, close to many main attractions, this hotel has 459 tastefully furnished rooms. Its excellent Fisk restaurant offers some of the city's finest seafood, while the Sky Bar features splendid views. $$$

Villa Källhagen
Djurgårdsbrunnsvägen 10
Tel: (08) 665 03 00
Fax: (08) 665 03 99
Villa@kallhagen.se
www.kallhagen.se
If you don't mind a 15-minute bus ride to the

centre and would enjoy Stockholm's maritime ambience, this is for you. It's a pleasant, modern hotel with 20 rooms, close to Brunnsviken Bay and Djurgården. The excellent restaurant is run by an award-winning chef. $$$

Birger Jarl Hotel
Tulegatan 8
Tel: (08) 674 1800
Fax: (08) 673 73 66
Info@birgerjarl.se/www.birgerjarl.se
This central hotel's recent facelift involved a host of Swedish designers and artists who gave it a nature-inspired look with an emphasis on birch wood. The workers overlooked Room No 247, however, which is preserved in 1970s style. The lobby of the hotel functions as a small gallery for Swedish art and handicrafts. $$$

Hotel J
Ellensviksv. 1 Nacka Strand
Tel. (08) 601 30 00
Fax: (08) 601 30 09
lena@hotelj.com
www.hotelj.com
Hotel J opened in 2000; 38 of its 45 rooms have waterfront views, 34 have a patio or balcony, all have clean, spare, wood furnishings. There are sports and leisure facilities nearby; the city centre is 15 minutes away. $$$

Långholmen Hotell
Gamla Kronohäktet, Långholmsmuren 20
Tel: (08) 720 85 00
Fax: (08) 720 85 75
Hotell@langholmen.com
www.langholmen.com
This hotel and conference centre is housed in a former prison building dating back to the 19th century. It is located on the leafy island of Långholmen in trendy Södermalm. The cells have been transformed into light, pleasant bedrooms with modern furnishings and all the usual facilities. The hotel has 89 single rooms and 13 doubles, all recently renovated. $$$.
From 25 June to 15 August it also functions as a youth hostel with 125 beds. $

Lord Nelson Hotel
Västerlånggatan 22
Tel: (08) 506 401 20
Fax: (08) 506 401 30
info@lord-nelson.se

www.lord-nelson.se

The Lord Nelson has the appearance of a maritime museum – exquisite nautical antiques adorn the rooms. The tall, narrow, 17th-century building even looks like a ship. It's small and cosy, and the 29 rooms are suprisingly light and airy given that buildings are so closely packed together in Gamla Stan. **$$$**

Rica City Hotel Gamla Stan

Lilla Nygatan 25
Tel: (08) 723 72 50
Fax: (08) 723 72 59
Info.gamlastan@rica.se
www.rica.se

Lots of atmosphere in a historic environment among the narrow streets of Gamla Stan, with the Royal Palace, Storkyrkan and the Houses of Parliament close by. The 51 rooms in this 17th-century building have recently been renovated to provide high-class comfort. There are conference facilities in the vaults. **$$$**

Rica City Hotel Kungsgatan

Kungsgatan 47
Tel: (08) 723 72 20
Fax: (08) 723 72 99
Info.kungsgatan@rica.se
www.rica.se

This newly built hotel occupies the five upper floors of the PUB department store building originating from 1876. Centrally located, with 270 modern, well-equipped rooms. **$$$**

Rica City Hotel Stockholm

Slöjdgatan 7
Tel: (08) 723 72 00
Fax: (08) 723 72 09
Info.stockholm@rica.se
www.rica.se

A first-class hotel offering peace and quiet in the heart of the city, near the colourful Hötorget marketplace, shopping areas, entertainment, and the Central Station. This 292-room hotel, built in 1982–4, offers a high standard and an international style. The buffet breakfast is served in a lovely winter garden; the lunch restaurant serves traditional Swedish food. **$$$**

First Hotel Amaranten

Kungsholmsgatan 31
Tel: (08) 692 52 00
Fax: (08) 652 62 48

Amaranten@firsthotels.se/www.firsthotels.com

Located in Kungsholmen, there is easy access from the hotel to the city centre by bus or on the subway. The excellent quality of the 423 rooms is enhanced by several bars and restaurants. It claims to serve Sweden's best breakfast. **$$**

Mälardrottningen Hotel and Restaurant

Riddarholmen
Tel: (08) 545 187 80
Fax: (08) 24 36 76
Reception@malardrottningen.se
www.malardrottningen.se

You would be hard-pressed to find more unusual and stylish accommodation than this luxury yacht (which once belonged to Barbara Hutton). It is moored at Riddarholmen, not far from Gamla Stan, and features 60 elegant, well-equipped rooms. The excellent restaurant is in a splendid setting for a sunset meal. **$$**

af Chapman & Skeppsholmen (STF/YHF)

Flaggmansvägen 8, Skeppsholmen
Tel. (08) 463 22 66
Fax: (08) 611 71 55
Info@chapman.stfturist.se
www.stfchapman.com

This would be a serious candidate for the title of the world's most beautiful youth hostel. Located on a gleaming white schooner moored off Skeppsholmen, the af Chapman has 136 beds and it also includes the 152-bed building facing the ship's gangway. Its café has become a favourite meeting place for a beer or coffee. The three-masted ship was named after the master shipbuilder Fredrik Henrik af Chapman. It was built in 1888 in the English port of Whitehaven and originally used as a freight vessel, only arriving in Sweden in 1915. **$**

Gustav af Klint

Stadsgårdskajen 153
Tel: (08) 640 40 77/78
Fax: (08) 640 640 16
www.gustafafklint.se

Moored at the foot of the Old Town, this is Stockholm's most centrally located hotel ship and youth hostel, and it is open 24 hours a day. The hotel features generously appointed rooms for 14 guests; the hostel accommodates 135 in two- or four-berth cabins. All cabins are above the waterline, many with portholes looking out across the bay towards Gröna Lund. **$**

Right: the *af Chapman* schooner – possibly the most beautiful youth hostel in the world

Mälaren-Den Röda Båten
Söder Mälarstrand, Kajplats 6
Tel: (08) 644 43 85
Fax: (08) 641 37 33
info@theredboat.com
www.theredboat.com
A cosy riverside hotel located at the point where Lake Mälaren meets the Baltic Sea in the heart of Stockholm, five minutes from the Old Town. In summer the floating restaurant Ludvigshafen offers a fine view. There are 90 beds in the youth hostel and four double rooms in the hotel. $

Tre Små Rum
Högbergsgatan 81
Tel: (08) 641 2371
Fax: (08) 642 88 08
Info@tresmarum.se
www.tresmarum.se
In this inexpensive but personal little hotel the guests prepare their own organic breakfast. There are now seven rooms – although it started out with three, hence the name Three Small Rooms – each comfortably and casually decorated to make it feel like home away from home. It's located in the heart of the fashionable, bohemian Södermalm district and the owner is usually happy to provide bicycles to guests who want to get around in quintessential Söder fashion. $

Zinkensdamm Vandrarhem (STF/YHF)
Zinkens väg 20
Tel: (08) 616 81 00
Fax: (08) 616 81 20
www.zinkensdamm.com
This, Stockholm's largest youth hostel, has 466 beds. It has an international clientele and a quiet location in the Tantolunden park area in Södermalm. It features a bistro and a pub. $

FURTHER READING

Insight Guide: Sweden, Apa Publications. A combination of detailed and insightful reporting on all facets of the country, complete with a photo-journalistic style of illustration.
Insight Guide: Scandinavia, Apa Publications. Comprehensive coverage of the whole of Scandinavia, including stunning photographs.
Sweden's History, Jörgen Weibull, Swedish Institute (www.si.se) A detailed account, from Swedish pre-history to the age of cyberspace by way of the Vikings.
Vikings, Carin Orrling, Swedish Institute. The writer, an archaeologist and art historian, paints a complex picture of the Vikings as navigators, craftsmen and traders as well as warriors and pirates. Handsomely illustrated.
Stockholm, Chad Ehlers, Bonniers. A veteran photographer of Stockholm, Ehlers captures the life and beauty of the city through all the seasons. A perfect gift or memento.
A Taste for All Seasons, Helena Dahlbäck Lutteman and Ingegerd Råman, Swedish Institute. The authors blend Swedish cuisine and design, composing menus and table decorations month by month, in a nicely photographed book.
The Stockholm Time Walk, Michael Tongue, Discovery Books. Fifty superb photographs of Stockholm, the oldest from the 1860s, arranged in a circular walk from Norrmalm, round Gamla Stan to Riddarholmen and Blasieholmen. Compare the views then and now.
Stockholm Horizons, Jeppe Wikström, Bokförlaget Max Ström. This enormous, beautifully photographed volume features both the familiar and surprising aspects of Stockholm's beauty. The author captures the essence of the city's neighbourhoods.

ACKNOWLEDGEMENTS

Photography	**Jan Lindblad Jr**
14T	**AKG London**
44	**LSH fotoavd/Hallwylska**
11, 46, 47	**Statens Historiska Museum**
14B	**Swedish Tourist Board**
Cover	**Torleif Svensson/The Stock Market**
Cartography	**Berndtson and Berndtson**
Cover Design	**Carlotta Junger**

© APA Publications GmbH & Co. Verlag KG Singapore Branch, Singapore

INDEX

Stockholm Transport

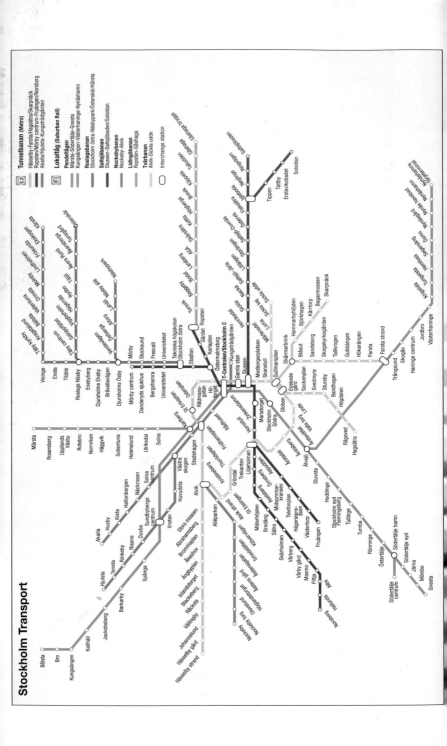

Tunnelbanan (Metro)
Hässelby–Farsta/Hagsätra/Skarpnäck
Ropsten/Mörby centrum–Fruängen/Norsborg
Akalla/Hjulsta–Kungsträdgården

Lokaltåg (Suburban Rail)

Pendeltågen
Märsta–Södertälje–Gnesta
Kungsängen–Västerhaninge–Nynäshamn

Roslagsbanan
Stockholm östra–Näsbypark/Österskär/Kårsta

Saltsjöbanan
Slussen–Saltsjöbaden/Solsidan

Nockebybanan
Nockeby–Alvik

Lidingöbanan
Ropsten–Gåshaga

Tvärbanan
Alvik–Sickla udde

○ Interchange station